Business Leaders:
MICHAEL DELL

Bu$ine$$ Leader$
MICHAEL DELL

Lauri S. Friedman

MORGAN REYNOLDS

PUBLISHING

Greensboro, North Carolina

Bu$ine$$ Leader$:

Russell Simmons
Steve Jobs
Oprah Winfrey
Warren Buffett
Michael Dell
Ralph Lauren
Faces Behind Beauty

BUSINESS LEADERS: MICHAEL DELL

Copyright © 2009 by Lauri S. Friedman

Library of Congress Cataloging-in-Publication Data

Friedman, Lauri S.
  Business leaders : Michael Dell / by Lauri S. Friedman.
    p. cm.
  Includes bibliographical references and index.
  ISBN-13: 978-1-59935-083-7
  ISBN-10: 1-59935-083-1
  1. Dell, Michael, 1965- 2. Dell Computer Corp--History. 3. Computer
industry--United States--Biography. I. Title.
HD9696.2.U62D454 2007
338.7'61004092--dc22
[B]

                                    2007049238

Printed in the United States of America
First Edition

Y921
Dell

Contents

Michael Dell *(Courtesy of Dell Inc.)*

ONE

A Business-Minded Boy

When Michael Dell was twelve years old, his favorite hobby was stamp collecting. He loved adding new, unique, and hard-to-find stamps to his growing collection, and was always excited at the prospect of learning more about stamps, where they came from, and how they were traded. Stamp collecting was not an unusual hobby for young people at the time. But unlike most other young stamp collectors, Michael turned a passionate hobby into a lucrative enterprise—before he was even a teenager.

As he enthusiastically collected stamps and read stamp journals, Michael learned more about how rare and unusual stamps were sold. The owners of valuable stamps typically paid an auctioneer or a stamp retailer a small fee to sell their stamps to other collectors. Stamp retailers also sometimes purchased stamps for their customers. These middlemen collected a fee for every stamp they bought or sold. This drove up prices for rare stamps, as stamp owners had to charge higher prices to account for the fees paid to auctioneers.

Instead of paying an auctioneer to buy and sell stamps for him, Michael decided to start his own business, creating an auction that took place through the mail. He convinced some neighbors and friends to consign their stamps to him, then placed an advertisement for the collection, which he called "Dell's Stamps," in *Linn's Stamp Journal*, a publication read by hobbyists. On an old typewriter, he pecked out a twelve-page catalog that featured all of the stamps in his possession and sent it through the mail to people who responded to his ad. When people bought the stamps, Michael made a small profit on each sale. In a short time the twelve-year-old boy had earned $2,000 by selling his stamps directly

When Michael was twelve years old, he started his own business selling rare stamps. *(Courtesy of Beaconstox/Alamy)*

to consumers. "I learned an early powerful lesson about the rewards of eliminating the middleman," Michael said of his stamp sale many years later. "I also learned that if you've got a good idea, it pays to do something about it."

Eliminating the middleman would become an important pillar of the Dell Computer Corporation, which Michael Dell would create just seven years after his stamp sale. Dell Computer's success was based on its direct-to-consumer model of business—selling computers directly to customers without the aid of a middleman such as a retail store. This model was revolutionary, and no other computer manufacturer had thought of it before, yet Michael Dell had stumbled upon the idea before he was a teenager.

Michael Saul Dell was born on February 23, 1965, into a middle-class Jewish family in Houston, Texas. He was the second of three sons born to orthodontist Alexander Dell and stockbroker Lorraine Dell. From this ordinary beginning Michael would one day become one of the richest men in the world, the youngest CEO to ever earn a ranking on the Fortune 500 list and a key figure in the computer revolution that continues to shape the lives of people all over the world.

Michael and his brothers, Steven and Adam, were competitive siblings who enjoyed playing ping-pong and other sports. Winning was important in the Dell household; when games got too rowdy, Alexander Dell would take his sons aside and scold them for playing too rough, but then remind each of them to do their best to win.

Even as a child Michael was interested in the business world. Michael was raised in a household in which business and current events were frequently discussed, making him comfortable with and interested in advanced topics at an early age. He recalls sitting at the dinner table, avidly listening to his mother and father explain the U.S. central banking system or talk about companies that might be good stock investments. He even had a checking account at the age of nine. "In our household," he said, "you couldn't help being aware of commercial opportunities."

Michael Dell would one day become known as the Henry Ford of the computer age—an allusion to the way he always sought the most efficient way to make and sell computers, just as Henry Ford had developed the assembly line to produce cars effectively and cheaply. And even as a young child, Michael was always looking for ways to eliminate steps that he thought were unnecessary. When he was in third grade he saw an advertisement in the back of a magazine offering a high school diploma in exchange for passing a test. Curious, Michael sent away for the test. "It's not like I had anything against school," he later wrote. "I really liked the third grade [but] if there was a way to get something done more quickly and easily, I wanted to try it. And trading nine years of school for 'one simple test' seemed like a pretty good idea to me." When the testing representative showed up at his house to administer the test, she was surprised to be greeted by an eight-year-old boy and his very confused parents.

When he was a teenager, Michael became interested in electronics. He was fascinated with figuring out how electronic gadgets worked. He enjoyed building radios from kits, for example, and was also interested in calculators because of their ability to do complicated math equations so rapidly. Math quickly became his favorite subject; he was in the advanced math track at school and was a member of the Number Sense

Early computers like the one pictured here were so large that they occupied entire rooms. *(Courtesy of U.S. Army)*

Club, an extracurricular activity in which students did complicated math problems in their heads and competed in math contests against other schools. Michael frequently stayed after school just to experiment with a newly installed teletype terminal, an early type of computer on which users could write simple programs or do calculations.

His interest in computers increased as he went through junior high and high school. Computers at the time were very different from the personal computers of today. When Michael was young, computers were huge, expensive systems that were usually owned only by universities, financial institutions, and large companies. Some of these computers were so big they took up entire rooms. Though technology gradually enabled computers to become smaller, the first predecessors to the personal computer were still large. These machines, called minicomputers, were often the size of a dresser or refrigerator, and cost tens of thousands of dollars.

But during the early 1970s a new technology called a microprocessor was developed. A microprocessor is a small electronic chip that contains transistors, which enable a device's electrical power to be used more efficiently. Using microprocessors, computer designers could dramatically reduce the size of a computer's central processing unit. Computers that once took up entire rooms could be shrunk to fit onto a desk. By the late 1970s, new machines known as "personal computers," or PCs, began to become available. These machines were small and reasonably priced, although very primitive compared to most home computers today.

One of the first personal computers that Michael got a chance to play with was a PC made by Radio Shack. It cost about $800 and was not very powerful. Unlike modern computers, which contain an internal hard disk drive, the Radio Shack PC required a bulky external cassette drive to store information. But Michael enjoyed playing around with the computer, and began writing programs in a simple computer language known as Basic. Using trial and error, he slowly learned how to write simple computer programs. He later said, "I was kind of fascinated with the computing power and what that could do and what that would mean. It was just an enchanting device for me."

Working on the computer made Michael feel like he was part of something important:

> [I was] just fascinated with a machine that could do so many computations so quickly. At the beginning of the genesis of the PC industry, it seemed like there was going to be a lot of excitement with [a] device like this, as it went into medicine and business and education and entertainment. Of course, nobody knew exactly what would happen, but it was a very exciting time.

Michael wanted to learn more about the way computers worked, so when he was fifteen years old he begged his parents to let him buy his own. He wanted the Apple II, a personal computer made by Apple Computer that was, at the time, the most popular PC on the market. His parents agreed

An Apple II computer *(Courtesy of AP Images/Eric Risberg)*

to get him the computer, but when the long-awaited machine arrived, neither of Michael's parents could guess what their son was about to do with it. He took the Apple II up to his room, laid it out on the floor, and promptly took it apart into hundreds of tiny pieces. They were infuriated.

But Michael had dismantled the computer to get a better understanding of how it worked. He soon learned how to not only put his Apple II back together again, but also how to make it work even better. He enhanced the computer by adding different pieces of hardware, experimenting with more memory, different disk drives, bigger monitors, and faster modems. He also experimented with different kinds of software, and eventually set up a bulletin board system (BBS) on which he could exchange messages with other computer users. The bulletin board system was a primitive version of today's Internet; by talking with other users over the BBS, Michael learned more and more about the way computers worked and were sold in the marketplace. He even started enhancing computers for his friends and neighbors, and began to consider trying to turn his love for computers into a business.

But before Michael could focus all his time on his computer projects, he had to get through high school. Although he was bright, he did not excel in his studies at Memorial High School in Houston. In fact, one of his teachers told him he would probably never go anywhere in life. Socially, Michael was considered a bit of a nerd. The photo in his 1983 high school yearbook shows him hunched over a computer, barely visible behind thick glasses. While he had friends, his interests always remained centered around electronic gadgets, computers, and seeking out new moneymaking opportunities.

Michael found one such opportunity when he was sixteen years old, while working a summer job selling newspaper subscriptions to the *Houston Post*. After selling subscriptions the way he had been told to do, by randomly calling telephone numbers, Michael realized there was a more efficient way to reach potential customers. After talking with people over the phone, he had identified two types of people who almost always bought newspaper subscriptions: newlyweds and people who had just moved into new homes. Instead of wasting his time calling people randomly, he decided to focus on those who were most likely to want them.

Michael learned that anyone who wanted to get married in Texas had to apply for a marriage license; the applications, which included contact information, were available to the public. He hired a few of his high school friends to collect the information. Michael also found that he could get lists of new home buyers from certain mortgage companies. Initially, he targeted the people who had purchased the most expensive houses, thinking they were wealthier and therefore more likely to have extra spending money. He sent each homeowner a personalized letter offering them a subscription to the paper. Michael's methods of targeting the most likely customers worked, and soon he was selling newspaper subscriptions by the thousands.

When school started in the fall, Michael was reluctant to give up the subscription-selling business. Though interested in academics, he was more motivated by the thought of earning money. He once said that it was his goal to "make more money than any other kid in school." So he continued to sell subscriptions after school and on weekends. One day, his economics teacher assigned his class to fill out the Internal

Revenue Service (IRS) paperwork for their tax returns as an exercise. While other students showed earnings of a few hundred dollars from babysitting jobs or working in fast food restaurants, Michael reported $18,000 in income from his newspaper subscription sales. At first the economics teacher thought the teen had miscalculated, and then she became depressed: at the age of seventeen, Michael had earned more than his teacher. Michael was even able to buy himself a BMW with the profits from selling newspaper subscriptions and enhanced computers.

Though Michael Dell had dreams of turning some of his ideas into a business, his parents had other plans for him. They felt it was important that their son go to college after he graduated from high school. They encouraged him to follow in his father Alexander's footsteps and become a doctor. Not wanting to disappoint them, Dell enrolled at the University of Texas at Austin, intending to study medicine and become a doctor. "Where I come from," he said, "not going to college is not an acceptable option." Dell started his freshman year of college in September 1983. But he could not give up his love of computers, and it would not be long before his dreams of owning his own business would come true.

TWO

Young Man, Young Company

While most college students his age were busy choosing their majors and spring break destinations, Michael Dell was more interested in tinkering with computers. He was often seen walking around campus with books in one hand and RAM chips in the other. In between classes he holed up in his dorm room (room 2713 of the Dobie Center), upgrading computers and selling them to lawyers, doctors, businesspeople, and students. "I liked Chinese food and electronic gadgets, and I never had enough spending money from my parents to satisfy these tastes," he said. "So I had to come up with a way to make my computer deliver the desired extras." He quickly gained a reputation for knowing how to fix and build quality personal computers.

Just three months into his freshman year of college, Dell was spending more time selling computers than attending class. He couldn't help it—selling computers fascinated and impassioned him. "I was fortunate to find my passion early in life," he commented. "[I] soon realized that all of those stacks of computer parts in my room were trying to tell me something. . . . I just knew there had to be something easier than organic chemistry!" Preferring his computer projects to his schoolwork, he rarely devoted time to his studies, and his grades began to fall. Concerned, his parents traveled from Houston to the campus in Austin to see what their son was doing. Dell barely had time to hide all the computers and parts behind the bathroom shower curtain before his parents walked into his room.

Despite his efforts to hide what he was doing, his parents quickly figured out what was going on. Alexander Dell told

A 1999 photo of Dell sitting in the dorm room where he started his business of upgrading and reselling computers. *(Courtesy of AP Images/ Harry Cabluck)*

him, "You've got to stop with this computer stuff and concentrate on school. Get your priorities straight. What do you want to do with your life?" Michael Dell immediately knew his answer. He told his parents: "I want to compete with IBM!" He knew that he wanted to build better computers than the computer giant IBM and change the way computers were sold by selling them directly to the customer instead of going through other channels.

But Dell's parents insisted that he needed to ditch his computer hobby and focus on his studies. So Dell made a deal with them: if he finished and passed all of his spring courses, he could run his computer business in the summer. Wanting to make them proud, Dell reluctantly stopped his dorm-room computer business—but only for three weeks. He just couldn't abandon what he felt was a winning idea: to build exceptional computers and sell them directly to customers. All around him, Dell saw the potential computers had for changing the world. "I knew that if you took this tool, previously in the hands of a select few," he said, "and made it available to every big business, small business, individual, and student, it could become the most important device of the century."

Dell also noticed a critical problem in the computer industry at that time and had ideas about how to fix it. Although personal computers were gaining popularity, the people running computer stores and repair shops didn't know much about the new machines. Many of them had previously sold televisions or stereo systems; to them, computers were simply another expensive high-tech product for sale. New computer users didn't know much about their machines either, and computer manufacturers such as IBM did not provide customer

Dell's goal was to compete with computer giant IBM. *(Courtesy of AP Images/Thomas Kienzle)*

support to help resolve computer problems. Dell recognized that offering helpful technical support from computer experts would be a great way to attract customers.

As the second semester of his freshman year began, Dell continued to sell computers unbeknownst to his parents, and even moved forward with plans to start an official business without their knowledge. He called his company PC's Limited, and registered it with the state of Texas in 1984. Then he placed an ad in the classified section of his local paper. With the advertising and the good reputation he had gained from previous customers, Dell soon had more business than he could handle. Still a college freshman, he was bringing in $50,000 to $80,000 a month selling computers out of his dorm room—more than the salary of many of his professors. To keep up with business, he eventually left the student dorms and rented a two-bedroom condo where he had more space for his computer parts. Nervous about how his parents would interpret the move, he waited for months to tell them.

Business kept growing, and shortly before final exams of his freshman year it became clear to Dell that if he was going to succeed, he would have to choose between pursuing a college degree and pursuing a business. In his heart, he wanted to follow his dream and compete with IBM to be the number-one personal computer manufacturer in the country. So at the age of eighteen, Dell dropped out of college to devote all his time to growing his computer business. "I just went ahead and did it," he later said. "Whatever the consequences."

Despite the fact that he never earned a college degree, Dell always retained a fondness for the University of Texas at Austin, which he credits with fostering his dreams and putting him in touch with the talented people with whom he would work for years. "Though I left UT prior to [graduating]," he said years later, "this school has been a big part of my life in many ways: as a source of guidance and counsel for a young start-up company, as a constant resource of talent and support for a growing and established business. . . . I feel a tremendous connection with this university."

Although Dell was at first nervous about abandoning a college education for an unknown future in the computer industry, looking back he knew it was the right decision. "I was in college for a year, so I got to experience many of the things people go to college for," he said. "The objective of going to college is to learn—and I think I've learned more doing what I've been doing than I ever could have in college."

In May 1984 he incorporated PC's Limited with just $1,000, the minimum required amount. He rented office space in Austin and hired a few people to take computer orders by telephone. Early operations were modest, he recalled: "manufacturing consisted of three guys with screwdrivers sitting at six-foot tables upgrading machines."

Soon Dell found an opportunity in the computer industry that proved to be very profitable. He took advantage of what was known as the "IBM gray market," which resulted from IBM's sales practices. IBM typically sold its computers to

Dell gives a speech during a ceremony to induct a PC's Limited computer from 1985 (foreground) into the Smithsonian Institution. *(Courtesy of AP Images/Jacquelyn Martin)*

resellers—big companies like Wal-Mart or specialized computer dealers—who in turn sold them to the end-users, their customers. Dealers had to place monthly orders with IBM, which had a factory that mass-produced computers; often, the dealers received more of the devices than they could sell before the end of the month. To get rid of this excess inventory, dealers sold the leftover computers at a reduced rate—and Michael Dell was there waiting to buy them. Dell and his employees upgraded the computers with better hard drives, extra memory, and other improvements, and then sold them at a profit. But Dell was troubled at the wasted energy and money expended on buying and improving these excess inventory computers. What if he could simply manufacture his own computers and sell them directly to customers? The more Dell thought about it, the more he knew that building his own machine was the best way to succeed. "It became very obvious," he said, "if we could design our own computers, and sell them directly to the customer with better support than the dealers offered, we would have an incredible business."

So Dell set to work designing his own personal computer. He hired a small team of computer engineers to build a unique machine that reduced the two hundred chips normally found in a PC to only five or six ASIC (application specific integrated circuit) chips. In-house workers assembled the machines, and telemarketers sold them directly to customers over the phone. Released in 1985, Dell's "Turbo PC" cost about $795, about 40 percent less than what IBM charged for its computers in the mid-1980s. The inexpensive and powerful new Turbo PC excited consumers, and in no time PC's Limited was selling more than a thousand each month.

Business was so great, in fact, that PC's Limited could not quite keep up with the demand. The 1,000-square-foot office space Dell had rented after leaving his dorm room at the University of Texas could no longer hold the operation. He moved into a second space that was more than twice the size, but after just five months it too was cramped and confining. A third move put the company into a 7,200-square-foot space, but six months later another move was necessary due to the tremendous growth of Dell's business. "We outgrew our telephone systems, our facilities, our organizational structures, every physical or electronic system we had," Dell said. In 1985 the company rented a 30,000-square-foot office space—the size of a football field—and still had to move again just two years later.

PC's Limited was doing millions of dollars of business a year, even though its owner was still too young to legally drink a beer. Dell's early days in business reflected his youth. Accustomed to a college schedule, he often overslept in the morning and found his employees hanging around outside his offices, waiting for him to show up and open the doors. "When I started the company," he remembers, "I rarely got the door open before nine-thirty. Then it was nine o'clock. Finally, we got started at eight a.m., and then I gave someone else the key."

He hired many of his college buddies to help out with his business, and though they maintained a productive atmosphere and worked hard, it was a casual, youthful, fun office. The first time PC's Limited sold more than $1 million worth of products in a single day, someone brought in cupcakes to celebrate, each decorated with "$1,000,000" written in icing. At other times, Dell and his employees cheerfully made do with limited resources. For example, during one period when money was tight, the company couldn't afford to buy trash cans, so employees used cardboard boxes that computer parts had been delivered in. During other periods of fiscal conservation, workers shared cubicles in an attempt to save space.

A spirit of youth, creativity, and adventure permeated the early days of PC's Limited. But Dell's youth threatened to become a handicap in the business world, where most company leaders and chief executive officers have years of professional experience. Although Dell's ideas and instincts were just as valid as an older businessperson's, potential collaborators did not always take him seriously. At one point Dell wanted to buy semiconductors, silicon chips that conduct electricity, to be installed in the computers. He asked for a meeting with executives at Intel, a high-tech company that manufactured semiconductors and microprocessors. But when Intel CEO Andy Grove learned he had a meeting with someone in his early twenties, he sharply asked his head of sales, "Why are you wasting my time with a child?"

The media, too, cast doubt on Dell's ability to run a company at such a young age. In 1988, when Michael Dell was twenty-three years old, *Forbes* magazine ran a story about him bitingly titled "Entrepreneur in Short Pants." And Dell often had to field questions from reporters about why he shouldn't be regarded as "just another soon-to-flame-out hotshot."

But Michael Dell handled such treatment with maturity and honesty, explaining to both reporters and business partners that his ideas were solid and profitable. Instead of a liability, Dell's youthful creativity and drive ultimately proved to be an asset in the business world. His enthusiasm for his work

Andy Grove *(Courtesy of AP Images/Paul Sakuma)*

and his confident belief that he could not fail gave his company the edge it needed. As Dell remarked later, "I didn't know all kinds of things, but that turned out to be strength. . . . Not being bound up by conventional wisdom can be extremely helpful."

THREE

Making Dell Different

In 1985 PC's Limited grossed about $6 million in sales. Over the next six years, however, Michael Dell's aggressive approach and adventurous spirit helped make his company one of the largest in the computer industry, increasing its annual sales to more than $500 million. Key to Michael Dell's success was the development of a few core strategies, which reflected his beliefs about the proper way to do business.

Dell's most revolutionary idea was adopting a direct sales model, eliminating resellers and selling directly to the customer. Dell believed that computer dealers, resale chain stores, and others who sold computers on behalf of manufacturers represented an unnecessary step that wasted money and clogged communication between the company and those who bought its products. Dell circumvented this traditional business practice by taking orders from customers directly, usually by phone. By 1987, Dell's telemarketers were fielding more than 1,700 calls about personal computers a day. Direct sales eliminated the need to maintain brick-and-mortar stores where customers would browse, as well as the need to pay resellers. "In one swoop," explained Joan Magretta in *Managing the New Economy*, "Dell eliminated the reseller's markup and the costs and risks associated with carrying large inventories of finished goods." Customers' orders were simply shipped straight from Dell's warehouse in Austin.

Because he had eliminated the middleman, Dell was able to sell quality computers at a much lower price than his competitors. In 1986, for example, IBM's personal computers containing the high-end Intel 386 microprocessor chip cost between $4,600 and $5,800. Similar computers from IBM's largest rival, Compaq, were priced slightly lower, between $4,300 and $5,000. But PC's Limited was able to offer its machines for between $2,500 and $3,900, an attractive difference.

The importance of the direct model to Dell's success cannot be understated. "When the company started, I don't think we knew how far the direct model could take us," Dell said. "It has provided a consistent underlying strategy for Dell despite a lot of change in our industry. . . . I don't think we could have created a $12 billion business [in 1997] in thirteen years [without it]."

Aiding in his success, Dell was not afraid to surround himself with executives who were older and had more experience than he did. The most important of these was E. Lee Walker, a forty-eight-year-old venture capitalist from Austin, who was hired as a consultant in 1986 and soon became Michael Dell's business mentor. Walker had been involved in numerous company startups, and understood the importance of good planning and proper financial management. "Lee helped me get around the potholes," Dell told *Forbes* in 1991. "Sometimes he was my father, sometimes he was my brother. We were very, very close."

Walker, who became president of the company in 1987, convinced Dell to change his company's name to Dell Computer Corporation. "Michael didn't want his name on the door," recalled Michelle Moore, the company's longtime director of public relations. "But Lee convinced him that if Dell was going to be a broad-based tech supplier, the name PC's Limited wasn't going to work. It took some doing."

Dell standing in his Austin computer factory in 1989 *(Courtesy of AP Images/Rebecca McEntee)*

Walker also brought several experienced, high-profile executives to the company's board of directors. These included Admiral Robert "Bobby" Inman, a former director of the U.S. Central Intelligence Agency (CIA), and George Kozmetsky, a founder of the industrial conglomerate Teledyne and the former dean of the business school at the University of Texas. Along with Walker, Dell's board provided helpful advice to the young entrepreneur.

Admiral Robert "Bobby" Inman was one of the high-profile executives who joined Dell's board of directors in 1987. *(Courtesy of AP Images/John Durcka)*

Nearly everyone who met the young computer company founder came away with respect for his exceptionally rich and quick intellect. "Of all the people I've worked with, he's one of a dozen or so extraordinarily fast learners," recalled Inman. "You didn't have to go through it a second time."

Another of Michael Dell's core maxims was to provide excellent customer service. As Dell had noticed in college, during the 1980s the computer industry had poor or nonexistent customer service. Computer users had no real knowledge about the machines they had purchased, and neither did most computer sellers. Meanwhile, computer manufacturers provided little or no customer support. "Very few business managers understood what 'system error' and other messages flashing across their monitors meant," explained business writer Nancy Koehn. "Few medium-sized and virtually no small companies had an IT department with a dedicated help desk."

Dell understood that helpful advice for customers could set his company apart from the competition. He hired support-staff personnel who thoroughly understood computers, so that they could best meet customers' needs. In fact, when first starting out, he made all the members of his sales force set up their own computers to develop a more intimate understanding of the products they were selling, and gain sympathy and insight into what a struggling, frustrated customer might be going through at home. "They probably didn't enjoy it," Dell said of his sales force, "but it gave them (and us) a real sense of what the uneducated customer would go through to set up his system. . . . As a result, they were able to help customers make informed decisions about what to buy *and* they could help solve equipment problems."

Dell speaks with a customer over the phone at a Dell call center.
(Courtesy of AP Images/Harry Cabluck)

Next, Dell created unique features to his customer-service program that would build Dell Computer's reputation and help earn it many prestigious awards. To make customers comfortable with buying computers over the phone and not in a store, Dell instituted a thirty-day money-back-guarantee on each computer, plus a one-year warranty, free on-site repair and customer support, and forty-eight-hour shipping for any necessary replacement parts. Dell also established a twenty-four-hour telephone hotline for product-related questions and comments, and a toll-free technical support hotline. If any customer had to wait more than five minutes to speak to a knowledgeable technician, Dell automatically mailed the customer a check for twenty-five dollars.

The impact of these strategies was enormous. According to Dell Computer's records, a full 90 percent of all customer phone calls were resolved to the customer's satisfaction within a single phone call. Dell's outstanding service led to one of the industry's highest rates of customer return: by the end of the 1980s, 70 percent of people who had purchased a Dell computer bought a second machine from the company, indicating a high level of customer satisfaction with the company's products and support.

In addition to helping people better understand their computers, Dell's commitment to customer service had another benefit: opening itself to customer comments gave the company insight into what customers actually wanted in a product. Unlike other computer manufacturers, who were prevented from communicating directly with customers because they dealt with retail stores and other middlemen, Dell was constantly provided by his customers with valuable information regarding what kinds of products to build, which to improve, and which to avoid.

Such insights led to Michael Dell's unique idea to tailor-make computers to each purchaser's needs. Dell machines are configured exactly to a customer's specification, increasing the variety in price and ability of each machine. Customers liked the flexibility of having many options for the characteristics of their computers, depending on what tasks they wanted them to perform. For example, an author working on a long book could order a computer with extra memory, while a large office that wanted employees to be able to pass files around easily could buy thirty computers with both floppy disk and hard disk drives.

The combination of giving customers exactly what they wanted at a low price was integral to Dell's early success. "Our close connection to our customers is one of the things we've become best known for at Dell," Michael Dell later commented. "When I first started the company, that 'direct link' distinguished us from our competition; helped us to determine where to best allocate our resources; and allowed us to provide the latest technology, a high-quality product, and great value."

Dell's products soon began to achieve widespread recognition as high-quality, affordable machines. Many of the products began winning industry awards, which further bolstered the company's reputation. "We began receiving five stars for quality, support, and service," remembered Dell. "All the key magazines began recommending Dell for best value and highest performance."

Michael Dell was not afraid of public scrutiny; he believed in his products. Therefore, in a particularly savvy move, he gave analysts for *PC Week, Computerworld, Byte, InfoWorld,* and other popular computer magazines the opportunity to personally test Dell computers. The positive reviews from these critics quickly translated into increased sales. For example, after *PC Week* praised Dell's first computer, Dell began selling more than one thousand Turbo PCs per month.

To grow even further, Dell decided to target large corporations to sell fifty or more computers at a time—the potential for revenue was enormous. Fueled by Michael Dell's determination, Dell Computer landed accounts to supply computers for some impressive outfits, including Dow Chemical Company, Continental Grain Company, airplane manufacturer Boeing, and financial giant Arthur Andersen. Supplying computers for such big clients helped boost the

During the late 1980s, Dell began to supply computers to large corporations such as the Dow Chemical Company. *(Courtesy of AP Images)*

Dell name and reputation for quality computers, and the strategy paid off tremendously. By 1991, almost half of all of Dell's sales were to major corporate, governmental, or educational customers.

A second critical decision was made during the late 1980s that would have a tremendous effect on Dell's success. Dell and his board of advisors decided to expand business to international markets. At the time, this was an uncommon move. Unlike today's globalized economy and marketplace, in the 1980s companies—especially growing ones like Dell—tended to stay within their own borders. But Dell was convinced that his strategies, which had proven successful in the United States, would work equally well in other industrialized nations.

Dell had first thought about international expansion while he was in college, during a family vacation in London. While his family was sightseeing, Dell took the opportunity to explore British computer stores. "I observed the same high markup/lousy service phenomenon in the United Kingdom as I had in the United States," said Dell. He thought that British customers would respond just as well as Americans had to buying computers directly from the manufacturer at a lower cost, all the while reaping customer service advantages.

Against this backdrop, Dell U.K. opened for business in June 1987, despite predictions of failure from the press. Dell remembers that all but one of the journalists who covered the opening of Dell U.K. predicted the enterprise would fail. But Dell's instincts about British consumers were correct. Computers flew off the shelves, and by the end of the century Dell U.K. was a nearly $2-billion-a-year company. From this success, Dell learned to trust his instincts, even

A Dell office building in Bracknell, U.K. *(Courtesy of Dell Inc.)*

if people told him he was crazy. "Sometimes it's better not to ask—or to listen—when people tell you something can't be done. I didn't ask for permission or approval. I just went ahead and did it."

Each of these moves resulted in outrageous growth for Dell. By the end of 1987, Dell was doing about $70 million in sales per year. The factory in Austin was churning out 7,000 customized, built-to-order machines a month. By the end of 1988, the company had more than doubled its 1987 sales, pulling in about $159 million in revenues that year. To keep up with this growth rate, Michael Dell decided to move his offices again, invest in extra manufacturing and warehouse facilities, and hire more employees.

The Dell Computer Corporation was one of the fastest-growing companies in American history, growing faster in its first few years than had such blue-chip companies as Wal-Mart, Microsoft, or General Electric. But all of this growth required the company to bring in more capital. The way companies usually do this is to "go public," meaning they sell shares of company stock that can be publicly traded on the stock market. In essence, shares of stock are like small pieces of a company that are bought by investors, or stockholders. The process of going public is a chance for stockholders to invest in a company, with the expectation that they will earn a return on their investment as the company grows and becomes more profitable. The company can use the money from stock sales to build up the business and make it more profitable.

Going public is a big decision for a company, and timing is crucial. If the company waits too long it could miss out on raising a lot of money; but if it goes public too early, it might not raise enough money to meet its needs and ensure continued growth. For these reasons, Dell was wary about taking the company public too soon. Instead, Lee Walker helped him sell a small block of Dell stock through the investment bank Goldman Sachs to a private group of investors. The timing was unfortunate—the sale came just a week after the October 19, 1987, stock market crash, at a time when the market was losing more than 20 percent of its value. However, despite the terrible market conditions, the sale was a great success. It brought in $21.5 million in working capital, and gave Dell experience working with external investors.

When Michael Dell decided to sell a larger block of shares in 1988, his decision to go public was met with initial skepticism. Financial analysts and business reporters were impressed by Dell's rapid growth, but few believed that the

in social situations. Friends credit Susan with helping to bring him out of his shell; she hosted parties at their home, which forced him to hone his social skills. "When you were talking to him, you almost had the sense he was going to wipe his shoes on the back of his pants," said one longtime acquaintance. "Susan was the wonderful impact there. Susan really did push him to get out and talk and to be comfortable at talking."

While he enjoyed and appreciated these changes, marriage did not distract Dell from continuing to build his company. In 1989 his company had sales of more than $300 million and was growing faster than practically all of its competitors. But despite his accomplishments, Michael Dell would soon be faced with challenges that would threaten his company's very existence.

FOUR

Ups and Downs

By the early 1990s the Dell Computer Corporation had exploded onto the personal computer scene. In its first four years of business, the company's annual sales rose at an impressive rate of about 250 percent each year. Dell Computer was turning heads everywhere from California to the United Kingdom. But shortly after establishing itself as a serious contender in the personal computer industry, Michael Dell and his company experienced a wave of bad luck that threatened to wipe the company out of existence. Dell would later blame this shaky period on his own poor judgment: he violated some of the core concepts on which he had founded his company and which had led to its success.

First, the company became stuck with a pile of computer chips that, due to technological advances, became nearly worthless overnight. In 1989 Michael Dell decided to buy

A memory chip

a large number of 256-kilobyte memory chips, anticipating that the chips would be in short supply in the coming year and that if his company was caught without an adequate supply it would limit the number of computers Dell could sell. "We bought as many of those suckers as we could get our hands on," he later noted. But soon after Dell made this purchase, manufacturers of memory chips discovered how to greatly increase their capacity, from 256K to one megabyte. (One megabyte is the equivalent of more than one thousand kilobytes.) Dell was suddenly stuck with millions of dollars' worth of worthless memory chips. Nobody would want to buy a Dell computer with a 256K memory chip when competitors' computers were so much more powerful.

To address this issue Dell had to make a few decisions that ended up further jeopardizing the company's image and reputation. The company had to sell the unwanted chips at a huge loss—about 70 percent less than it had paid for them—which cut deeply into sales revenue. Another consequence was that Dell, which had built its reputation by promising computers at the best value, was forced to raise prices to make up for the money it had lost on the chips. One observer called Michael's memory chip problem "the company's biggest mistake to date."

On the heels of the inventory crisis, the company weathered another problem. This time, it was a family of products called Olympic that, despite the investment of a lot of time and effort by Dell's research and development (R&D) staff, did not ever make it to the marketplace. In 1989 Michael had come up with the idea for the Olympic product line—desktop and workstation computers that featured flashy new technology capable of performing many tasks—believing that it would be Dell's best product ever. However, he had failed to follow one of his most important maxims: always listen to customers *before* building a product. Although the Olympic products were technologically impressive, Dell Computer's customers simply did not need such complicated machines.

Michael dryly described the typical response to the product line: "'Some things are compelling. But the whole product in and of itself isn't compelling *enough*. I'll pass.'" It was the company's biggest failure. The problems depressed Dell's profits significantly, even though the company's overall sales continued to rise, reaching $388 million for the 1990 fiscal year. However, Dell Computer only showed a profit of $5.1 million, down from $14.4 million in profit in 1989. Stockholders earned just a penny on every share, a disappointment to the market as the company's stock price had risen rapidly since Dell Computer became a publicly traded company.

However, Michael Dell made the right decisions to put his company back on track. "We made some mistakes, but we also had the strength to work our way out," he told *Nation's Business*, a publication of the U.S. Chamber of Commerce, in April 1991. "We now work more closely with out suppliers and maintain only a ten-week supply of parts. Our real mistake in R&D would have been to make the [Olympic computer] when we found there was no market." Some of Dell's other decisions during this time—including expanding his company's overseas presence into France, Germany, Sweden, and Italy—also helped improve the company's bottom line.

As a result, Dell Computer rebounded strongly in the 1991 fiscal year, posting a profit of $27.2 million. Overall sales were up 41 percent, from $388 million in 1990 to $546 million in 1991. Also in 1991, Dell Computer received the top ranking for customer satisfaction among business users in a survey taken by the prestigious research group J. D. Power and Associates.

Dell computers coming off the production line at a Dell factory. *(Courtesy of Dell Inc.)*

In just a few years, Dell Computer had grown tremendously, jumping from the twenty-second largest personal computer company in the United States in 1989 to fifth largest in 1991. Michael Dell was doing well. His 35 percent stake in Dell Computer was worth an estimated $300 million, giving him a place on the Forbes 400 list of the wealthiest Americans, and in 1992 he became the youngest CEO ever to head a Fortune 500 company. By the next year, Dell Computer's annual sales had soared to $2.9 billion.

Around that time, though, the company hit another rough patch. In the early 1990s laptops, or notebook computers, were

A Dell laptop
(Courtesy of Dell Inc.)

a fast-growing segment of the personal computer industry, and Dell was interested in expanding into that market. However, he made a crucial mistake when he assigned the company's desktop computer design team to design Dell Computer's laptops. Although the desktop computer engineers were a talented group, creating a high-end laptop computer required a wholly different approach. The designs they came up with were flawed and sold poorly.

As the laptop division struggled to produce a quality computer, Michael Dell hired an experienced notebook engineer named John Medica to oversee development of Dell's laptops. Before coming to Dell, Medica had helped to develop Apple's laptop computers, which were considered among the best in the industry. Unfortunately, Medica felt that only one of Dell's laptop designs seemed to have any possibility of succeeding against the competition. Although it was a painful and costly move, Dell took Medica's recommendation and canceled most of the products that were in development. "We could not sell something that wasn't ready and that our customers wouldn't like," he later said. At the time, however, Dell was stunned and upset. "Michael was mortified. He was really shaken up by this," recalled Carl Everett, the former head of sales for chipmaker Intel. Millions of dollars of inventory, as well as tens of millions more in research and development costs, had to be written off, and for the first time Dell Computer showed a loss for the year. In addition, the company lost market share to rival Gateway, dropping to sixth among U.S. manufacturers.

Around the same time, Dell put an end to his company's short-lived attempt to sell computers through retail stores. Although Dell's direct sales model was well known and

The Dell offices in Round Rock, Texas *(Courtesy of Dell Inc.)*

admired in the computer industry, during the early 1990s the company had faced growing pressure from shareholders to gain access to a previously untapped market—the small businesses and household consumers who shopped for computers at retail stores like Sam's Club and Wal-Mart, or at computer chains like CompUSA. In 1990, for example, the discount retailers Sam's Club and Price Club had generated more than $1.6 billion in computer sales. Dell Computer executives wanted to be part of this buying frenzy, and Michael Dell reluctantly agreed to try selling Dell computers in the retail marketplace.

When the retail sales program began, however, financial analysis showed that Dell had made a mistake. Although Dell was selling a lot of computers, the company was actually losing money on retail sales, as too much of the profit from each sale went to the retailer, not the manufacturer. "We'd have meetings and everyone in the room would say we're doing great," Dell said, "and then you'd look at the numbers and there were problems. We had businesses that were performing extremely well and businesses that were performing extremely poorly, but nobody really knew which was which."

Michael Dell and others began to have other reservations about the retail sales program. He became concerned that relying on salespeople that Dell had not trained would hurt the company's image. Worse, by selling through a third party Dell Computer was not able to communicate with the people who purchased its computers, and without customer feedback Dell Computer would receive no direction with regard to which products to continue making and what new ideas the company should pursue.

Michael
Dell in 1994
(Courtesy of
Paul Harris/
Online USA/
Getty Images)

Just months after he had announced that Dell computers would be sold through Wal-Mart, Michael Dell pulled the plug on the idea. It was a decision that was difficult for him to make. Everyone around him—the media, industry analysts, and even some executives within his own company—told Dell he was making a mistake. Retail was the future, they said, and Dell would severely limit its growth if it did not participate.

Between the laptop problems and the retail debacle, it seemed that the future of Dell Computer Corporation might be in doubt. For the first time, Michael Dell—at age twenty-eight still a young man by the standards of the business world—felt the weight of his responsibility. "In early 1993, I felt as if every piece of news I got was bad," he remembered. Although he had approached Dell's growth periods with confidence and aplomb, now he felt unsure of his ability and even a little frightened. Dell's stock price had fallen, the company was getting negative press, and some critics seemed to gloat that wonder boy Michael Dell had simply been a flash in the pan. "Today people sometimes ask me if, during this time, I was scared," he said. "Of course I was. Having disappointed our customers, employees, and shareholders, I was worried about losing their trust. But I was also scared because, for the first time, I started thinking I might be in over my head."

Dell was going to have to learn quickly from his mistakes in order to get his company back on the right track. Fortunately, reacting to change had always been one of his strong suits, and as he solved the problems he also learned how to avoid such problems in the future. Dell knew the best way to earn back the trust of customers was to be honest with them about the problems and let them know he was doing his best to resolve them. He worked with Dell's notebook group to create a quality product and kept customers informed of the process the whole time. Many customers appreciated this, seeing it as a personal courtesy rarely extended to customers by big businesses. Dell explained:

> Because we laid out our plan to correct the problem to our customers and shareholders in a clear, straightforward manner, we never lost their trust. We went to each customer affected by the notebook situation and made it right. We said, "We're bringing out a new line. Here's our phased strategy and our service and support plan. Here's why you shouldn't be nervous about doing business with us." People were genuinely blown away by that.

The plan was for John Medica to concentrate on perfecting Dell's one remaining laptop model, which became the Latitude XP. Medica developed a solid machine that featured Intel's speedy 486 microprocessor, a color display, and a thin, light frame that was comparable to other laptops. Most importantly, the machines included an amazing new technology—lithium-ion batteries, which were smaller and ran longer than other companies' laptop batteries at the time.

Michael Dell had learned about lithium ion batteries during a business trip to Japan in January 1993. He recalls a Japanese man from Sony running up to him in a convention center asking him to take a minute to discuss energy power systems. "Energy power systems?" thought Dell. "Is this guy going to try to sell me a power plant?" But the man wanted to show Dell a new technology that used lithium ion to make long-lasting batteries. The man said that they were more powerful than batteries made from nickel, which were found in most notebook computers. Knowing that if he could increase the battery life in Dell's notebooks he could capture a larger share of the market, Dell listened. Lithium ion batteries were lighter and more compact than conventional batteries, the man said, and had the potential to last up to twice as long. At the time, laptops were primarily used by businesspeople while traveling, so such an increase in battery life was an important consideration.

Though it sounded good, Dell was hesitant—to put new technology into an entire line of computers is no small decision. But Dell was persuaded when he learned that Sony was the only company making these batteries. If Dell bought Sony's entire supply, there would be none for the competition. If lithium-ion batteries worked, his notebooks would be lighter and run longer than other manufacturers' laptops, and there would be nothing his competitors could do about it in the short term.

Dell therefore decided to use the batteries in the Latitude XP. To generate publicity before the new product was launched in August 1994, Dell and his team cooked up a spectacular public-relations event that would showcase the new laptop's battery power. They invited top industry analysts and journalists on a cross-country flight from New York to Los Angeles. At the beginning of the flight, Michael gave each guest a Latitude XP and invited them to check out the computers. At the end of the flight, six hours later, the computers were still running. They had broken every record for laptop battery life on the books.

Although the decision to shut down Dell's notebook production while the product line was revamped had been costly, in the long run it proved to be the correct move for Computer. The Latitude XP became one of the best-selling laptops, and gave Dell Computer its first significant share of the laptop computer market.

At the same time, although pulling out of retail unnerved many of Michael Dell's colleagues, it turned out to be a solid decision for Dell Computer. Sales continued to soar as the company returned to the direct model, which would serve Dell well for many more years. The company went from a $36-million loss in fiscal 1993 to a profit of more than $130 million in fiscal 1994, with gross sales of $3.4 billion that year. "Dell [Computers] had the opportunity to learn . . . big lessons . . . the hard way," Dell said in a 2003 speech at the University of Texas at Austin. "But . . . we fixed our problems as fast as we found them." For all of these efforts, Michael Dell was named "Turnaround CEO of the Year" by *Upside* Magazine. The award recognized the obstacles Dell Computer had faced and the tremendous effort Dell had made in getting his company back on track.

FIVE

Racing at the Speed of "Dell-ocity"

Michael Dell and the Dell Computer Corporation had experienced some serious problems in the early 1990s. But by spending time thoroughly fixing each problem, and also by returning to the core maxims on which he had originally founded Dell, Michael was able to get his company back on track. And get back on track he did—by the end of the century, Dell was poised to realize his longtime goal of challenging mainstream computer giants such as IBM, and to make his business model world renowned.

One reason for the turnaround was that Dell recognized that his management approach was not working. In a very short time, the company had grown large: from $388 million in sales in 1990 to more than $2 billion in sales by 1993. However, Dell and his managers had always focused on increasing the company's sales, without considering profitability and other factors. This single-minded focus on growth meant the management team had a hard time adapting to problems related to the company's larger size. Dell found that his managers could not even determine which products were profitable and which were not, and began to feel that he was losing control of the company. Dell recalled:

> One of the things that is confusing and almost intoxicating when you are growing a business is that you really have little way of determining what the problems are. You had different parts of the company believing they were making their plan, but when you rolled up the results of the company, you had a big problem. It was symptomatic of not understanding the relationship between costs and revenues and profits within the different lines of the business.

To turn things around, Dell began assembling a new team of managers, whom he recruited from such high-tech firms as Motorola, Hewlett-Packard, and Apple. The most important hire was Mort Topfer, the former head of Motorola's paging business, to reorganize and oversee the day-to-day operations at Dell. Topfer quickly restructured the company's administration and implemented tools that would permit greater planning and sharing of financial information among key managers.

Another person Dell brought in to help right the company was a consultant named Kevin Rollins, a partner in the firm Bain and Company. Bain had become one of the most sought-after consulting firms in the United States because it not only developed management strategies and corporate plans, it sent people like Rollins in to oversee the implementation of those plans. Rollins's specialty was in the high-tech area, and Dell found that they worked well together. In 1996 he

Mort Topfer *(Courtesy of Phil Walter/Getty Images)*

convinced Rollins to leave Bain for a high-level executive
position with Dell Computer, as director of the company's
sales in the United States.

Dell's willingness to share power with people who knew
the ins and outs of business better than he did has been a

Kevin Rollins *(Courtesy of Dell Inc.)*

hallmark of his business career. Throughout the history of Dell Computer, Michael Dell has not hesitated to add older, more experienced colleagues to his employee roster. He has always recognized the benefits of surrounding himself with smart, creative people who understood the business and could help improve his company's performance. "I didn't know everything there was to know about running a large business like this," Dell admitted. "But I knew how to hire people who did." One of Michael Dell's key consultants during its growth period agrees. Mort Meyerson, who was Dell's closest advisor from 1988 to 1992, commented, "He didn't try to run [the company] himself. . . . That's where [a lot of] CEO/founders fail."

Personally, although things at Dell Computer were up-and-down in 1993, Michael Dell's personal life was going well. That year, Susan Dell gave birth to the couple's first child, Kira. However, a scary moment occurred a few months after the birth, when a burglar broke into the Dells' Northwest Hills home. Michael and Susan Dell were not there, but the baby was home with a nanny. No one was hurt, but the Dells were shaken by the incident. ("I'm fearful all the time," Susan Dell told the judge at the burglar's trial.)

The Dells soon commissioned construction of a new $18 million mansion atop Thompson Mountain, a nearby peak that offered panoramic views of the Austin area. The 22,000-square-foot house—popularly known in Austin as "the castle"—is one of the largest homes in the world. It has eight bedrooms, eight full bathrooms, an exercise room and two swimming pools to help the Dells keep fit, and a five-level terraced lawn. For business purposes, the house also contains a conference room. The house is secluded, surrounded by sixty acres of woodlands and protected by a tall fence and a legion of security guards. Dell, who typically refuses to speak about his personal life, had little to say about the new home. "The house is a place where we live," he told *Texas Monthly.* "It's a sort of private place. If you drive by the house, you'll notice that it's placed in such a way that it's not particularly easy to see, and quite frankly, that was somewhat intentional."

Although just the taxes on the property would be more than $230,000 a year, the Dells would not have any difficulty paying their bills. After overcoming the problems of 1993, Dell Computer saw its business surge over the next few years. The company's continued growth was fueled in part by an innovation that was just beginning to come to the attention of computer-savvy Americans: the Internet, an electronic network that could carry information from all around the world.

In the early 1990s, however, people were still experimenting with how to use the network. Until 1993, no technology existed that would allow users to access information in a simple, standardized way; that year, researchers at the University of Illinois Urbana-Champaign created what became known as the Mosaic browser, a sophisticated computer program that provided a standardized Internet interface accessible by any user. Suddenly, users could transmit information across the Internet without needing to know how to write software, or even very much about how to use computers at all.

From the moment the Mosaic browser was introduced, Dell sensed a great opportunity. "I was enthralled by the concept [of the Internet]," he explained. "I loved the idea of

being able to turn on a PC and see what was going on anywhere in the world. As soon as I could get my hands on it, I
installed the Mosaic browser on a machine in my house, and
would spend tons of time on the Internet every night after
my kids had gone to sleep."

In its early days, the Internet was not used for the
same kinds of things it is today. A few companies created
Web sites, where they posted information like company
histories, annual reports, or press releases. Initially, not
many products were sold online. Graphics were unso-
phisticated—many Web sites did not even feature pic-
tures—and most corporate executives felt customers would
not want to purchase products they could not feel or see.
Furthermore, transferring credit card information over a
computer seemed unsafe, as encryption technology was
not yet advanced enough to allow secure transmissions.
For these reasons, many retailers did not immediately recognize the Internet for the powerful marketing and selling
tool it would become. Instead, visitors to their Web sites
were directed to nearby stores or to the company's toll-
free sales number.

Unlike most other companies, however, Dell Computer
was uniquely poised to take advantage of Internet sales.
The company had already managed to sell products that
customers couldn't see or hold—Dell's entire business was
conducted over the phone. And Michael Dell was not dis-
suaded by the fact that few expensive products were sold
online. "If you could order a T-shirt online, you could order
anything—including a computer," Dell believed. "And
the great thing was, you needed a computer to do this! I
couldn't imagine a more powerful creation for extending

our business." To Dell, the Internet represented not a new, unfamiliar horizon, but a cheaper, more efficient extension of selling directly to the consumer—the ultimate direct sales tool.

Dell launched its Web site, www.dell.com, in June 1994. In addition to product information, the Web site allowed customers to order computers online. A calculator enabled customers to determine the cost of various combinations of parts in their Dell computers. The Internet allowed Dell Computer to do its job more efficiently, as information that had once been transmitted over telephone lines or fax machines could now be transmitted through the Internet. Communication between Dell and its customers became cheaper and more efficient overnight. A Dell customer could log onto the company's Web site, select a customized computer system, enter a credit card number, and complete his or her purchase in less than twenty minutes. The new computer would be delivered to the customer's doorstep in a matter of days.

Although today online ordering is common, in the early 1990s the concept was revolutionary, and it helped Dell climb to the top of the PC industry. The results were well received by many different observers, with numerous business journalists or financial experts noting, "Dell has been positioned for something like this since its beginning."

Soon after the debut of www.dell.com, the company's sales began growing 20 percent each month. By 1996 Dell was selling more than $1 million in merchandise over the Internet per day. Later that year Dell introduced its first custom-made Web links for customers. Called "Premier Pages," the links allowed customers to tap directly into the company's service and support databases and retrieve personally customized information. The Premier Pages feature further solidified Dell's reputation for customer service. By 1999, Internet sales topped $35 million per day, and by the next year they were more than $40 million per day.

After years of suspicion that Michael Dell was a young flash in the pan, and that his company's unique model would fizzle out, Michael had proven to the world that he was a

Dell with Dell computers in 1997 *(Courtesy of AP Images/RIchard Drew)*

competitor to be taken seriously. Customers weren't the only ones noticing Dell's achievements: financial investors, journalists, politicians, and others eventually realized that Dell was doing something different—and it was working. In 1996 Dell's profits grew 91 percent, and its sales increased to $7.7 billion. "For Dell, the online world promises even greater speed and cost savings," wrote Gary Williams in *Business Week*. "With Dell racing past rivals like Sunday drivers on the Information Highway, there may be a new pace for manufacturers in the age of the Internet: Dell-ocity."

Realizing that the Internet transcended all national borders, Michael Dell decided to further expand and sell Dell computers all over the world. With Dell UK, the company had successfully experimented with international business, and now Dell believed that the Internet would make greater international sales possible. He was right. By 1996, the company was selling more than $1 billion wealth of computers to European consumers, and by 1999 Dell was selling to customers in more than 170 nations.

To deal with the increased growth, the company began opening manufacturing plants outside of the United States. Mort Topfer, who was given so much authority that Dell sometimes referred to him as a "co-CEO," had encouraged Dell to open a factory in Penang, Malaysia, in 1995. Five years later, Dell employed more than 36,000 people in thirty-three countries. The company had manufacturing centers in the United States, the United Kingdom, Ireland, Malaysia, China, and Brazil, and customer support call centers in India, China, Morocco, Panama, the Philippines, the Czech Republic, Canada, and El Salvador.

The Dell center in China *(Courtesy of Dell Inc.)*

Although Michael Dell credited his new managers for the company's turnaround, he was often the person who came up with the key ideas and decisions. For example, it had been his idea to sell computers through the Internet, and he pushed ahead despite the reservations expressed by some of his key managers. "I don't think Michael gets enough credit," Mort Topfer said. "He has an incredible sense of the market. And he has created every element of the Dell model."

Although Dell attempts not to micromanage his employees, he does pay attention to the day-to-day details, and that has also helped to make his company better. For example, in the mid-1990s Dell decided that it was necessary to reduce the company's "failure rate"—the percentage of computers returned because they did not work properly. Even though Dell's failure rate was among the lowest in the industry, Michael Dell wanted to do better. Ultimately, he decided that the hard drive, perhaps the most sensitive part of a PC, was being handled too much—more than thirty times during the computer-assembly process. It cost a significant amount of money to redesign the company's production lines, but this cut the number of "touches" to less than fifteen. Once this was done, Dell's failure rate for computers dropped by 20 percent, which resulted in a significant cost savings and a better reaction from customers.

Dell also decided to position his company to gain a share of the market for computer file servers. Unlike PCs, which are connected to monitors and are used by one person at a time, file servers are powerful computers that can be used to store application programs and data files. Multiple users can be linked by a network to the server, and can log in to access files and programs. Servers are also required to host Web sites and run Internet applications. Michael Dell felt there were several good reasons for his company to expand into this market:

A Dell file server
(Courtesy of Dell Inc.)

> The first reason was that our corporate customers wanted one vendor for all products. So if you had just desktops and notebooks, you were going to get in trouble with those accounts. The second problem was that our competitors had enormous profits in servers, and they were overcharging customers for servers and using those excess profits to compete with us in desktops and notebooks. So we said, "We've got to put an end to this. We're going to go into the server market and take away the profit havens of our competitors."

Although Dell is serious when it comes to his business, his friends and acquaintances describe him as a funny person with a dry sense of humor and a zest for life. He has often tried to make Dell Computer a fun, imaginative place to work. For example, when the company was unveiling its servers in 1996, a huge promotional event was held in an auditorium in Austin before 7,000 spectators. Michael Dell opened the event by running into the auditorium carrying an Olympic-sized torch, and subsequently entertained the audience as master of ceremonies. Another gimmick that drew laughs was "Server Man," a superhero figure complete with a cloak, tights, and a big red "S" on the front of his shirt.

Expanding into the growing market for powerful servers was a necessary move for Dell. By the late 1990s the market for personal computers began to level off, as greater numbers of consumers purchased the machines. By 1998, overall PC sales in the United States had fallen by 3.5 percent. Although Dell's sales continued to increase, new markets were needed to maintain the company's rate of growth. With their higher prices (high-end Dell servers cost $600,000, which was still considerably lower than the servers sold by rival Sun Microsystems), servers offered higher profit margins than

PCs. Dell's competitive prices enabled it to increase its share of the server market from 2 percent in 1996 to 24 percent just four years later.

The success of Dell Computer made Michael Dell, at just thirty-two years old, the wealthiest man in Texas and one of the hundred richest men in the world in 1997. The 16 percent stake that he still owned in the company was valued at more than $4.3 billion. But Michael Dell was not through yet; even bigger things were still ahead.

SIX

Reaching the Top

I n 1998 Michael Dell finally realized a lifelong dream: to beat the personal computer giant IBM. Early that year Dell Computer surpassed IBM as the third-largest supplier of notebook computers in the United States, according to market research firm International Data Corporation (IDC). The excellent performance, attractive design, and reasonable price of the Dell laptops, along with the company's outstanding customer support and service, were all listed by IDC as reasons for the takeover. Overall, the company was ranked fourth among PC manufacturers, with about an 8 percent share of the market for worldwide PC sales.

Dell was not through by any means, however. The market for personal computers had grown stagnant, so larger PC makers like Compaq, IBM, and Hewlett-Packard saw their profits drop significantly in 1998. They were forced to slash their prices by nearly 25 percent to sell their machines.

Dell speaking at a conference in 2000 *(Courtesy of AP Images/Mark J. Terrill)*

However, even with the price cuts Dell Computer's machines were cheaper than the competition. This was because Dell's direct sales model eliminated the dealer markup that added to other companies' prices, and its built-to-order system meant that the company's factories did not produce any extra inventory. These advantages enabled Dell to seize large chunks of market share from its larger rivals. By the end of 1999, Dell had surpassed IBM, Hewlett-Packard, and Compaq to become the largest computer seller in the United States with sales of $25 billion. Although Compaq remained the world sales leader, clearly Dell had its rival in its sights.

That same year, Dell collaborated with Catherine Fredman, an experienced business writer, to write a book about himself and his company's climb to the top of the PC industry. Reviewers found *Direct from Dell: Strategies that Revolutionized an Industry* an engaging account of Michael's experiences building his corporation. The book was a bestseller, although Dell donated most of the proceeds to a charity for children.

Indeed, as Michael Dell's personal fortune grew he began using a larger share of his wealth to help others. In 1999, he and his wife established the Michael and Susan Dell Foundation. With an endowment of more than $1 billion donated by the Dells, the Dell Foundation is one of America's largest charities.

In an interview, Dell explained that he wanted to begin using his money to improve people's lives while he was still around, to direct the funding to worthwhile causes and to see its effects. "A bunch of guys sitting around trying to decide what we want to have done with our money after we're dead, that's not a very good idea," said Dell. "Maybe they would

Beginning in the late 1990s, Dell and his wife, Susan, began using a part of their wealth for the betterment of others. *(Courtesy of AP Images)*

have wanted this. No, maybe they would have wanted that. Maybe we want this. No, no, no. Forget all that. We're going to do this while we're still here and get it right."

Michael and Susan Dell agreed that the charitable programs their foundation would support must have a lasting and meaningful impact on peoples' lives. "Giving isn't just about forking over money and saying, 'See you later,'" Michael Dell explained. "It's about making sure that you're getting the desired outcome." During its first seven years, the foundation committed more than $300 million to funding projects that help the underprivileged.

Michael Dell also began to become more involved in political causes during this time. A devout Republican, he donated considerable sums to the Republican Party in the late 1990s, and in 2000 he was a part of a group of high-

Dell (first row, second from the right) stands with other technology leaders during a conference with President Bush. *(Courtesy of AP Images/J. Scott Applewhite)*

profile Republican business leaders who contributed a total of $1.6 million to George W. Bush's presidential campaign. After the election, when confusion over vote tabulations in Florida led to a two-month-long stalemate as the ballots were recounted, Dell joined other executives in signing a letter that urged the Democratic Party's candidate, former vice president Al Gore, to concede the election. The letter, dated December 5, 2000, read, "We understand that some of your advisors may be urging you to fight to the bitter end. We call upon you to voluntarily concede this close-fought election . . . for the betterment of the country." As a thank you for his efforts during the electoral campaign, Dell was invited to Bush's inaugural ball. At the ball, President Bush's twin daughters wore gowns designed by Susan Dell.

The Dells continued to maintain close ties with the Bush administration after the 2000 election. Michael Dell was appointed to the President's Council of Advisors on Science and Technology. This council had been formed in 1990 by the president's father, to "enable the President to receive advice from the private sector and academic community on technology, scientific research priorities, and math and science education." (It is reported that George W. Bush has even called Dell to ask technical questions about his computer.) Susan Dell was appointed to the President's Council on Physical Fitness and Sports, a volunteer government committee that, according to its Web site, "serves as a catalyst to promote health, physical activity, fitness, and enjoyment for people of all ages, backgrounds, and abilities through participation in physical activity and sports."

But these other endeavors did not distract Michael Dell from his focus on his business. Dell continued to batter the competition, especially in the online arena, and gained market share as a result. On April 19, 2001, Dell Computer Corporation became the world's largest PC maker, with 12.8 percent of the global market compared to 12.1 percent for Compaq. (By this time IBM had fallen to fourth place globally, with only about 6.2 percent of the market share.)

Michael Dell had aimed for the top and had finally reached his goal. He later spoke about the importance of setting goals:

> Set your sights high and achieve your dreams and do it with integrity, character, and love. And each day that you're moving toward your dreams without compromising who you are, you're *winning*. [At times] you might think of yourself as just a number. However, I recommend that you choose the number one.

With the success of Dell's strategies confirmed, other business leaders began commenting admiringly on his methods. "Occasionally, rarely, history is made when a gifted new leader, who has a vision of new processes and technologies, produces a brilliant new business model," observed Ford Motor Company CEO Jacques Nasser. "Henry Ford did it in automobiles, Michael Dell has done it in PCs." Consultants Fons Trompenaars and Charles Hampden-Turner credited Michael for "brilliantly and intuitively [solving] several crucial dilemmas facing the computer industry." And many people remained in awe of how much Dell had accomplished at such a young age. "It's like watching Michael Jordan stuff the basketball," says Steven Milunovich, a top executive at Merrill Lynch. "I see it. I understand it. But I can't do it."

But Michael Dell was not content to rest on his laurels. Overall computer sales remained flat in 1999 and 2000, and although Dell continued to be profitable, to keep sales increasing the company needed to find new markets—such as the market for servers, which Dell had entered a few years earlier. By 2000 Dell was the second-largest provider of servers running Windows software and using Intel chips (sometimes called Wintel servers, to differentiate from the proprietary systems sold by Sun Microsystems, IBM, and other manufacturers).

Another area in which Dell looked to become involved was in Internet services such as Web hosting. Dell Ventures, a firm that would provide venture-capital financing to enable small but promising high-tech companies to grow, was formed in 1999. Within two years, Dell Ventures had invested more than $700 million in more than ninety companies, forming strategic partnerships that, Michael Dell hoped, would help to fuel Dell's growth. For example, in January 2000 Dell Ventures purchased a stake in Interliant, a New York-based Web hosting company. The next month, Dell Computer began offering Interliant's services to its customers. As an article in *Forbes* explained, Dell reaped numerous benefits from this deal. "First, Dell steers customers to Interliant and takes a cut," explained business writer Daniel Lyons. "Next, Dell sells its servers to Interliant to support those new customers. Finally, Dell's support boosts Interliant's sales, which should drive up the value of Dell's stake."

But even investments like this could not keep Dell Computer's growth from slowing. The company reported earnings of $32 billion for the 2001 fiscal year (which ended in December 2000), up from the previous fiscal year's $25 billion; however, financial analysts and stock market experts were disappointed to see its growth rate drop from more than 50 percent to less than 30 percent. Partly as a result of this decline—and partly because of an overall drop in stock prices after March 2000 that became known as the "bursting of the dot-com bubble"—the value of Dell's stock dropped by nearly 50 percent, to twenty-four dollars per share in November 2000.

Michael Dell was not concerned. He explained in interviews that the drop was partly due to the weak market for PCs, and partly because as a company gets larger, it becomes more and more difficult to sustain high growth rates. "Adding $7 billion to $25 billion in revenues for most companies would be a cause for celebration," he said. In fact, the entrepreneur saw the depressed state of the PC market as an opportunity to seize a larger share of the market from his competitors.

In late 2000 Dell started a price war by slashing the cost of its machines. For Dell, this represented a win-win opportunity. If a competitor tried to maintain their market share by matching Dell's prices, it would lose considerable amounts of money because of its higher operating costs. If competitors ignored Dell's gambit, his company would be in a good position to gain an even larger share of the PC market.

Many stock market experts admired the move. "He had more to lose than at any time in his career," commented Don Young, a former financial analyst for the investment banking firm USB Warburg. "Dell bet the company that they would take (market) share and their competitors would not match it. . . . They were right. It was the boldest move they've ever done." Despite the risks, for Dell it was an easy decision. "We're a growth company, and we're on the attack," he told reporters.

The approach succeeded dramatically. In 2001 Dell Computer was practically the only PC maker to show a profit, earning $1.7 billion on sales of $32 billion. At the same time Dell's share of the U.S. computer market grew to more than 25 percent, and it surpassed Compaq as the number-one seller of Wintel servers. Dell's success led to his selection, by *Chief Executive* magazine, as CEO of the Year.

It seemed as though nothing could stop Dell Computer from complete domination of the PC industry. Then, in the spring of 2002, two of Dell's largest rivals, Hewlett-Packard and Compaq, joined forces in an enormous $23 billion deal— the largest merger in the history of the computer industry. Initially, the new Hewlett-Packard (the Compaq name was

A Dell printer *(Courtesy of Dell Inc.)*

dropped from the new company) surpassed Dell as the world's largest PC maker.

But many people were not sure whether the arrangement was a good idea. "Your competitors want this deal to go through," former GE chairman Jack Welch warned Hewlett-Packard's Carly Fiorina during a CNBC interview. "It will create chaos. They will clean both your clocks while you're doing all this." Michael Dell and his team certainly saw things that way. Dell saw an increase in its business with several large corporations, which were concerned about the effects of the Hewlett-Packard/Compaq merger. "More and more doors are opening up to us," commented Dell president Kevin Rollins.

One area where Dell hoped to compete directly with Hewlett-Packard was in the sale of peripheral devices, particularly ink-jet and laser printers. Hewlett-Packard controlled more than 50 percent of the printer market in 2002, and cash from this division of its business enabled the company to continue making PCs even when they were not profitable, such as during the price war with Dell. The most lucrative part of the printer business, however, was not the machines that actually did the printing; it was the expensive ink or toner cartridges that the machines used. A person who purchased a Hewlett-Packard printer could be expected to purchase numerous highly profitable cartridges for that machine over several years.

In 2003 Dell introduced inkjet and laser printer lines that were priced lower than its competitors; Dell's ink and toner cartridges were also significantly less expensive than other manufacturers (in the case of Hewlett-Packard, about 45 percent cheaper), although they were still slightly profitable for Dell to produce. Printers quickly grew into a significant business for the company—within two years, Dell had captured 20 percent of the market.

To reflect Dell's transition from a company that primarily sold personal computers to one that offered other high-tech products, such as printers, servers, and even some consumer products like flat-panel televisions, in 2003 the company's name was officially changed from Dell Computer Corporation to Dell Inc.

A bigger change was on the way, however. On March 4, 2004, Michael Dell stepped down as chief executive of Dell Inc., saying that he wanted to have more time to spend with his family. His replacement as CEO was his close friend Kevin Rollins, who had started working at Dell in 1996 and had served as its president. The two executives had worked closely together for several years, and Dell—who would retain his position as chairman of Dell's board of directors, as well as the company's primary shareholder—promised to stay involved in the company. "I've still got the same great job," Dell told *Fortune* in April 2004. "We run the business together, and we're going to continue. But I thought it was appropriate to publicly recognize Kevin's achievements and capabilities. So he is the CEO now."

Rollins admitted not feeling any concern that Dell would be looking over his shoulder. "People don't realize that the way Michael and I have been running the company was irrespective of titles," he explained. "We just worried about what needs to be done and who's available. When Michael talked to me about the CEO job, my first reaction was to ask, 'You're not going to do anything different as part of the deal, right?' I wasn't interested in having a lot more to do.

It's a big company, growing very rapidly, and it takes two of us to do it."

Michael Dell was turning over the reins while his company was on top of the computer world. Dell's direct sales model and its built-to-order approach enabled the company to dominate worldwide PC sales, and it seemed to be successfully moving into other high-tech areas as well. With Michael Dell having become an internationally famous multibillionaire before the age of forty, no one could blame him for wanting to ease his heavy work schedule and devote greater attention to his personal life.

SEVEN

A Private Man

Although Michael Dell relinquished his CEO position to spend more time with his family, he does not enjoy talking about what he does when he's not at work. In fact, Dell is intensely private; he even had to be persuaded to put his name on his company during the 1980s.

"I don't have any desire to expose a great deal about my personal life," he told an interviewer from *Texas Monthly*. "There's an over fascination with certain things that don't necessarily have to do with whether a company is succeeding. And ways of characterizing things in convenient buckets that make people feel good because it sounds like it ought to be true."

Occasionally, though, Dell will let some personal details slip. For example, he has said that his typical day begins around 6 A.M., when he wakes and exercises. Dell enjoys swimming, lifting weights, horseback riding, and jogging—he can run a

A view of downtown Austin, Texas. Dell lives near Austin, and the Dell Foundation supports a number of local causes there.

mile in less than seven minutes—and in the winter, he and his wife Susan enjoy taking skiing vacations. With Dell's competitive spirit, it is not surprising that he also enjoys playing sports such as racquetball or basketball. "I like any good competitive game where there's a lot of noise and smashing things," he said. Others can attest to this; Tom Meredith, former chief financial officer at Dell Inc., once described Dell as having "an in-your-face desire to win."

Dell likes to make his children breakfast before dropping them off at school. After that daily chore, Dell goes to work. He spends at least two hours a day reading and answering e-mails—he once estimated that he gets about 175 e-mails a day, and answers at least sixty of them. When he gets home from his workday at about 6:30 P.M., he enjoys unwinding with his kids and eating dinner as a family. Then he makes time to read to his children before tucking them into bed. Once they're asleep, he uses the quiet time to catch up on work and e-mails.

Susan and Michael Dell have four children—Kira, Alexa, Juliette and Zachary. Michael Dell's family takes first priority in his life—despite his busy schedule, it is said that he never misses his son's baseball games. Says Mark Tebbe, a longtime colleague, "He is extremely family oriented. He's got a great family life." When asked his favorite place in the whole world, Dell repeatedly answers, "Home."

Like her husband, Susan Dell is an entrepreneur. In the 1990s she started designing expensive evening gowns. In 1997 she founded a fashion company, Susan Dell Inc., and two years later she opened a clothing boutique in the Austin neighborhood of Westlake. In 2004 she began producing a line of clothing for the fashion label *Phi*, which is sold through Neiman Marcus department stores.

Susan Dell is also a dedicated athlete who has competed in a variety of events, including the New York City Marathon and the Ironman Triathalon. When she ran the marathon in 2001, Michael Dell followed her progress as she ran, taking cabs to checkpoints along the streets of New York in order to cheer her on.

Although friends agree that Susan Dell has helped her husband open up socially, his natural tendency toward introversion has occasionally caused problems at work. For example, in 2001, internal surveys filled out by Dell Computer employees revealed that Michael Dell's subordinates considered him impersonal and emotionally detached. Dell was disturbed by these reports, and he made an effort to improve his demeanor at work. He gathered his top twenty managers together and made a speech admitting that he was shy, and acknowledging that his aloof persona affected the workplace. The speech was videotaped and circulated to all Dell employees. "It was powerful stuff," said Brian Wood, a Dell executive. "You could tell it wasn't easy for him." Although making this admission was difficult, the speech did seem to improve Dell's image among his employees.

Michael Dell is not shy, however, when it comes to his business goals. He has a reputation as an aggressive, hardnosed negotiator. One magazine dubbed him the "bogeyman of the PC industry" because of his unrelenting quest for market domination. Dell once commented that if any animal could symbolize Dell Inc., he would like it to be a shark, explaining, "It's the biggest, baddest, meanest beast in the ocean, and it gobbles up its competitors." Michael also admits to having little patience for error—when mistakes occur, he does not accept excuses. "There's no 'The dog ate my homework' here," he says of the atmosphere at Dell. However, Michael does try to keep his aggressive tendencies under control. He keeps a plastic toy bulldozer on his desk, for example, to remind himself not to steamroll over people.

Michael's personal shyness is one reason for his intense desire for privacy. Another is an unwillingness to subject his family to the public spotlight unnecessarily. "It's not relevant, really," he says about details of his personal life. "I can't imagine why anyone would care."

He is, however, more than willing to share his ideas about what makes a business succeed. Dell has often said that an important key to success is to ignore conventional wisdom. Although it is important to listen to other peoples' opinions, he believes, it is best to implement a good idea without worrying that it might fail. Had he obeyed the conventional wisdom of the computer world in the early 1980s, he might have never come up with his unique ways of building and selling computers. At various times executives with greater business experience told Michael Dell that such ideas as selling computers over the Internet, or extending direct sales into foreign countries, would never work. "It's fun to do things that people don't think are possible or likely. It's also exciting to achieve the unexpected," he wrote in his bestselling 1999 book *Direct from Dell*.

Michael Dell exudes self-confidence and urges other would-be entrepreneurs to do the same. "Believe in what you're doing," he advises. "If you've got an idea that's really powerful, you've just got to ignore the people who tell you it won't work, and . . . embrace your vision."

At the same time, one of Michael Dell's more admirable traits is that, unlike some other high-profile corporate CEOs, he is not an egomaniac. Instead, Dell has shown that he is willing to listen to other points of view. Throughout his company's history, he has been willing to surround himself with talented people and learn from those who had more knowledge of the industry than he. In a 1988 profile in *Forbes*, Stanley Angrist observed, "Probably the smartest thing [Michael] Dell has done is recognize the limits of his business experience, compensating for that weakness by surrounding himself with older men."

Although after more than twenty years in business Dell certainly has plenty of experience, he remains proud of his ability to work with others and to consider a variety of opinions. "Try never to be the smartest person in the room," he advised the graduating class at the University of Texas at Austin in a 2003 speech. "And if you are, I suggest you invite smarter people . . . or find a different room. . . . We are all gifts to each other, and my own growth as a leader has shown me again and again that the most rewarding experiences come from my relationships."

Dell is an entrepreneur at heart, and he enjoys finding new opportunities to invest his vast wealth. He owns a 377-room luxury Four Seasons resort in Maui, Hawaii, and also owns stakes in the car rental chain Dollar Thrifty and the restaurant chains Steak n Shake and International House of Pancakes. But although Dell's money is invested in these

Dell has invested his money in a number of other companies, including the International House of Pancakes. *(Courtesy of AP Images/ Nick Ut)*

properties, he does not take the same day-to-day interest in them that he does with Dell Inc.

Even after relinquishing the CEO position, Dell remained committed to seeing the company he founded grow and succeed. To stay on top of things, he tried to personally use as many of Dell's new products as he could. "Dell produces an awful lot of products now, so I can't possibly try out every one of them," he said. "But I certainly make it my business to use as many as possible as they are being developed. I want to test the stuff out to make sure it works. And of course, you gotta have the latest stuff. The coolest stuff." Dell has remained concerned about what his customers think, and he often visits Internet sites on which Dell customers discuss the company's products. "I go to the Usenet forums, the chat rooms," he said. "I learn about things we are doing well. I learn when we screw up."

Aside from his responsibilities on the Dell board, Michael is an active participant in other organizations. He serves on the Foundation Board of the World Economic Forum, and on the executive committee of the International Business Council. He is a member of the U.S. Business Council and continues to serve on the U.S. President's Council of Advisors on Science and Technology. He also sits on the governing board of the Indian School of Business in Hyderabad, India.

Michael and Susan Dell have also continued to donate generously to charitable causes through the Dell Foundation. Many of its grants focus its efforts on improving the health and education of children and young adults. One program that exemplifies this goal is Dell Scholars, a scholarship fund that was established in 2004. The program provides $20,000 scholarships to financially challenged but talented

Dell speaking at the World Economic Forum *(Courtesy of AP Images/Michel Euler)*

high-school students, so that they can earn college degrees. "The Foundation's mission [is] to reach underserved students who are academically prepared and college ready, and to provide them with scholarship funds to achieve a college education," the Web site for the Dell Scholars program notes. Since the program's inception, more than $5 million in scholarships has been distributed to help cover educational expenses for more than 250 students.

Aside from Dell Scholars, the Dell Foundation donates money to help other charitable and cultural organizations. Many of these groups are local: recipients of Dell Foundation grants include the Austin Children's Museum, the Long Center for the Performing Arts, the San Antonio Area Foundation, Ballet Austin, the Jewish Community Association of Austin, the Austin Community Foundation, the Austin Habitat for Humanity chapter, and the Austin Shakespeare Festival, among hundreds of other organizations. The gifts reflect Michael and Susan Dell's desire to invest in their home community.

But the Dell Foundation has also donated to national and international groups and causes. It has given hundreds of thousands of dollars to Heifer International, which provides valuable livestock to poor rural families all over the world, particularly in African nations. It has worked through Kids Alive International to provide support for orphaned children in Kenya and Sudan, and has given nearly $500,000 to the Glimmer of Hope Foundation to bring clean water to rural Ethiopia.

In India, where Dell Inc. has a manufacturing facility and a call center, the Dell Foundation has focused on improving the lives of children in urban slums, where large numbers of poor people live in crowded, unsanitary conditions. Dell Foundation programs in cities like Delhi and Hyderabad provide access to clean water and sewerage facilities, improve the quality of education, and provide job training for thousands of Indians. The Dell Foundation has also donated to organizations that work in Iraq, China, Sri Lanka, Indonesia, the Maldives, and Bangladesh.

Michael Dell approaches charitable giving in much the same way he approaches business: he wants to see a good return on his investment. As a result, the Dell Foundation thoroughly researches each charity before selecting it as a partner. "It's really easy to hand over your money and feel like you've done your duty," he says. "But that's no solution. Find out what, exactly, is going to happen with the funds that you give to an organization. What has that organization's productivity been in the past? Does it have a team and an infrastructure to make good use of the money? You make more progress if you hold people accountable and measure their results. So if you're going to get involved with something, make sure that you're getting your expected outcome as a return on your investment." Another way that the Dell Foundation helps stretch its dollars is by promising matching grants. The Dells challenge other wealthy philanthropists to put up money for a particular cause, program, or event. If they do, the Dell Foundation will match, dollar-for-dollar, the amount they pledge.

In addition to these programs, the Dell Foundation has lent a hand in times of crisis and disaster. When a massive tsunami devastated coastal areas of Indonesia and other countries of the Indian Ocean in December 2004, killing more than 230,000 people in ten nations, the Dell Foundation donated millions to groups assisting with the relief efforts. After Hurricane Katrina devastated the Gulf Coast of the United States in September 2005, the foundation provided a great deal of money to cleanup and relief efforts. "I'm a pretty results-oriented guy," explained Dell. "If I'm going to give away some money, I want something good to happen rather than just people feeling good for a while. I want something really good to happen."

Although Michael Dell has become known for his philanthropy, his greatest accomplishment to date has been the

After a massive tsunami hit Indonesia in 2004, the Dell Foundation donated millions of dollars to aid relief efforts. *(Courtesy of AP Images/ Gemunu Amarasinghe)*

development and refining of his direct-sales model, which revolutionized PC sales. As a result, he holds a place in history as the youngest CEO ever to have his company make the Fortune 500 list. He has been named "Entrepreneur of the Year" by *Inc.* magazine, "Top CEO in American Business" by *Worth* Magazine, and "CEO of the Year" by *Financial World* and *Industry Week* magazines. In November 2001, *PC Magazine* recognized him with a Lifetime Achievement Award for having ideas that "defined an industry." And the Consumer Electronics Association (CEA) gave Dell the 2007 Digital Patriot Award for his lifelong contributions to technological innovation and for his championing of the consumer electronics industry. "Michael Dell has changed access to consumer technology through his incredible vision, persistence and unwavering dedication," said Gary Shapiro, president of CEA, also calling him an "industry pioneer who continuously fights for innovation."

"There's always a better way to build a computer, or map a genome, or liberate a country, or take a basketball team to the Final Four," Michael Dell told the Austin graduates in 2003, advising them to "work to understand the world around you. Read books. Read websites. Read other people. Circle the pitfalls and highlight the opportunities. Then build a vision of how it could all be better and work like hell to make it happen."

EIGHT

Back in Charge

Although Michael Dell stepped down from his position as CEO of Dell Inc. in 2004, he remained chairman of the company's board, as well as its largest shareholder. As a result, he continued to be involved in overseeing the company's operations. Several initiatives that Dell proposed as board chairman proved successful and also brought the company excellent publicity. One of these was a plan that would enable Dell customers to recycle their old electronic products free of charge.

Often, older computers or consumer electronic devices are simply discarded when their owners buy newer, more powerful models. Unfortunately, computers, printers, cell phones, and other electronic devices contain components that are poisonous to the environment or take thousands of years to decompose, and pollution from these devices has become an increasingly serious problem.

Dell workers picking up computer equipment to recycle (*Courtesy of Dell Inc./Business Wire/Getty Images*)

At the turn of the century Dell Computer started to become more sensitive to environmental concerns. Michael Dell wanted his company's products to be made with the environment in mind: constructed to conserve energy and last as long as possible with a minimum impact on the earth. For example, Dell stopped using plastics that contain brominated flame retardant chemicals (BFRs), because when these plastics are discarded they leech poison into groundwater.

In 2005 Dell started a program that invited customers to turn in their old machines for recycling, regardless of whether they had purchased a replacement computer from Dell. The company even promised to pick up computers from consumer's homes. Computers that were not functional would be broken down into components that could be recycled, thus minimizing the impact on the environment. If their older computers still worked, Dell invited people to donate them to the National Cristina Foundation, which helps the disabled and economically disadvantaged. The Dell Foundation would arrange to pick up computers at people's homes, refurbish them, and redistribute them among the needy—all free of charge thanks to grants and gifts provided by Dell.

Dell's efforts to protect the environment have not gone unnoticed or unrewarded. In 2007, the Sierra Club classified the company as a "Forward Green Leader"—one of the nation's top five environmentally progressive companies. Greenpeace International's "Guide to Greener Electronics" consistently ranks Dell Inc. among the top five environmentally friendly technology companies. The company has also received special attention and praise from the Electronics Products Environmental Assessment Tool (EPEAT), a system that rates different types of computers based on categories such as recyclable components, efficiency, and lack of harmful materials. Dell was one of the first electronics manufacturers to register products with EPEAT, and many of its products have been labeled as above-average examples of products built with the environment in mind.

Another Dell initiative was considered by some observers unwise, but to Michael Dell it fit the philosophies he had held since he was young: defy conventional wisdom, and do what feels right. In 2005 Dell Inc. opened a new computer assembly plant near Winston-Salem, North Carolina. The decision

The Dell plant in Winston-Salem, North Carolina *(Courtesy of Dell Inc.)*

received a lot of media attention because many American companies—including Dell—have moved their manufacturing operations overseas to save money. But Michael Dell believed this new facility, which would create thousands of new jobs, could be cost-effective by reducing the company's shipping costs to consumers on the East Coast. "Our business in North America continues to grow in increments of $6 billion to $7 billion a year—but where are you going to make all the stuff?" Dell explained in *Fortune*. "With our business model, it just does not make sense [to go off-shore]. The value equation is better building close to the customer." Dell Inc. also received more than $200 million in state and county tax incentives for locating the new facility in North Carolina.

Dell's continuing success was striking, especially when compared to other computer manufacturers. By mid-2005 IBM had given up making personal computers, selling its PC division to the Chinese firm Lenovo. Stock in Gateway, which had once traded at more than $80 a share, had fallen to less than $5. Compaq, once the world's largest PC maker, sold out to Hewlett-Packard; although this move initially pumped up Hewlett-Packard's stock price, soon the new company was floundering. The Hewlett-Packard/Compaq merger did not prevent Dell from surpassing the larger company in global sales, and by mid-2005 Dell Inc. had taken the top position, with nearly 18 percent of all computers sold worldwide. Business analysts agreed that the mid-2000s were a terrible time to be in the computer business—unless you were Michael Dell. "You have to just say he has done a hell of a job," Jack Welch, the former CEO of General Electric and one of the most respected corporate leaders in American business, told *Fortune*. "No one has pulled the levers of cost, quality, and service better than [Michael] Dell." As a result of Dell's leadership and vision, in 2005 Dell Inc. was named "America's Most Admired Company" by *Fortune* magazine.

But the sweet taste of victory would soon turn sour for Dell, as a series of crises in 2006 threatened to derail the company's growth. An especially troublesome problem emerged in late 2005, as reports began to surface that some Dell laptops had suddenly burst into flames. The problem, it turned out, was with the rechargeable lithium ion batteries, which can spontaneously combust when damaged or short-circuited. Dell computers were not the only machines to use lithium-ion batteries—since being introduced by Dell they have become an industry standard, and are used in other manufacturers' computers, as well as in mp3 players, personal digital assistants (PDAs), and cell phones. However, Dell apparently had received a batch of damaged batteries,

Defective lithium-ion batteries caused problems for Dell Inc. in 2005–06.
(Courtesy of AP Images/Matt Slocum)

which had caused the problem—as well as a massive public-relations nightmare for the company.

Sony, which had manufactured the batteries, claimed that the fires were occurring because of the way Dell had constructed its computers, but Michael Dell was quick to reject this suggestion. "We know exactly why there was a problem. Sony had contaminated its cells in the manufacturing process," he insisted. "The batteries were contaminated, and were no good no matter what you did with them." Dell Inc. quickly addressed the problem, and in December 2005 the company recalled 35,000 laptop batteries that were thought to pose a risk. Affected customers were promised safe replacements free of charge.

Although it was hoped that this initial recall would take care of the problem, this was not the case. In July 2006 an office building in Illinois had to be evacuated when a worker's Dell laptop caught fire. In another incident, a Dell laptop burst into flames during a conference in Osaka, Japan. This incident had been captured on video and was soon posted on the Internet, bringing the problem significant public attention and leading to widespread industry speculation that Dell's laptops were dangerous.

A similar incident occurred in Singapore in July 2006. A man was working late in the office when his computer, running on battery power, suddenly began to make what he described as popping noises. "White smoke began to pour out of the machine, completely filling up the room, and there were flames coming up the sides of the laptop," he said. The man told reporters that he grabbed the machine by its screen and tossed it in a sink full of water to douse the flames, but the laptop continued to smolder. Although the man survived the incident unharmed, he told reporters he could easily have been burned or otherwise injured. "I'm now so paranoid that it will happen again that I don't use my laptop on flights anymore," he said shortly after the fire. "Just imagine if that had happened on an aircraft."

In August 2006, Dell recalled approximately 4.1 million laptop batteries to prevent additional battery fires. But just one week later, another catastrophic fire broke out. This fire, which occurred in the Florida home of a man named Louis Minnear, was said to have been caused when a Dell laptop was set on a pile of papers on the living room sofa. The house was completely engulfed within about twenty minutes; although no one was killed, the Minnear family lost nearly all of their possessions.

The battery-fire problem became a favorite scandal in the high-tech world, causing both the company and its founder great embarrassment. During a public-relations trip to Australia, where several laptops had immolated, the press lambasted Michael Dell for having little to say about the problem or for responding to pointed questions with brush-off answers such as "Customers can always contact us" or a terse "No comment."

At the same time, Dell's growth continued to slow as the demand for personal computers remained stagnant. To offset this weakening of its traditional revenue source Dell attempted to expand into the manufacture of consumer electronics. However, this foray was received poorly. In 2005 Dell introduced an mp3 player, the DJ Ditty, that executives hoped would rival the popularity of Apple Computer's iPod, the dominant music player on the market. The player was a disappointing flop and was soon discontinued. Similarly,

Dell's line of flat-panel televisions, which displayed music, movies, and photos from computer screens, compared unfavorably to models manufactured by Hewlett-Packard and other rivals.

With more competitors adopting direct sales along with their retail sales, some analysts even began to question whether Dell's traditional direct-sales approach could continue to reap profits. A 2006 article in *Business Week* explained, "It's becoming harder for Dell to run one of its most profitable plays: luring customers to its Web site with cheapo

Dell holds the DJ Ditty, an mp3 player introduced by Dell in 2005. *(Courtesy of AP Images/Joe Cavaretta)*

models and then getting them to buy a $2,500 box with all the bells and whistles." For the first time in the company's history, Dell's actual earnings fell below expectations for several consecutive quarters. In the third quarter of 2006, for example, Dell reported that its earnings had dropped by 46 percent from the previous year.

The *Business Week* article went on to say that the summer of 2006 had been "one mishap after another" for Dell: "a massive recall of potentially self-igniting laptop batteries, a dismal earnings report, and an announcement that the computer maker is under Securities and Exchange Commission scrutiny for the way it counts revenues." In November 2006, Dell admitted that the Securities and Exchange Commission (SEC), an agency of the U.S. government that oversees corporations that are traded publicly on the stock market, had started a formal investigation into the company's accounting practices. The company promised to cooperate with the government investigation, eventually releasing a detailed explanation of accounting errors and restating four years worth of financial statements.

Even though Dell Inc. still earned more than $3 billion in profit in 2006, the company's lower overall earnings and its various public-relations nightmares made customers, employees, and investors wonder how Dell would recover. Perhaps most galling of all, by the end of 2006 Dell had lost its title as the world's number-one PC seller to Hewlett-Packard.

In the face of these problems, Michael Dell urged the company's board to remove Kevin Rollins as CEO. On January 31, 2007, Rollins resigned from Dell, and by the next day Michael Dell found himself back where he began, as his company's chief executive officer. In the press release announcing Michael Dell's return, board director Samuel A. Nunn stated: "Michael's vision and leadership are critical. . . . There is no better person in the world to run Dell at this time."

Michael Dell immediately began announcing changes that he hoped would get Dell Inc. back on track. Perhaps the most dramatic of these changes was a decision to try selling computers through retail stores again. This strategy surprised many analysts, particularly because Michael Dell had often commented that the company's previous foray into retail sales had been a mistake. However, although Dell had no intention of abandoning the direct-sales model that had made his company successful, he believed the move into retail was warranted because Dell Inc.'s competitors had copied his methods and were starting to become more successful with their own direct sales. "The direct model is not a religion," Dell explained. "It's a great strategy, works well; there are things we can do with it. But that's not the only thing we can do as a company." In June 2007 several Dell computer models became available in thousands of Wal-Mart and Sam's Club stores in the United States, Puerto Rico, and Canada.

Dell also attempted to remind the world that, despite Dell Inc.'s problems, the company has a bright future. From 2001 to 2006 it was the number-one seller of personal computers in the world. Although it lost that title, Dell continued to run second to Hewlett-Packard and in 2007 gained back a chunk of the market share it had lost. Dell also remains the top PC vendor in the U.S. market, with nearly 29 percent of all computers sold. By the end of 2007 Dell had 88,100 employees, nine manufacturing sites worldwide, and worked with more than eight hundred suppliers.

When one interviewer asked Michael Dell to look ahead at the future of personal computers, the entrepreneur admitted being excited about potential new developments and what they will mean for his company. Dell said that he believes the PC will continue to be an integral part of everyday life, and that it will grow in its importance and diversity. "What you are going to see," he said about future technology, "[is] all these different shapes and forms and sizes and workstations and portables, big ones and small ones and multiple processors and single processors and handheld machines and all sorts of varieties. . . . The PC is an indispensable part of how productivity and entertainment, education, [and] medicine works today in society." If the past is any indication, Michael Dell will remain an integral part of future technological innovations.

Michael Dell is a billionaire entrepreneur, award-winning CEO, advisor, committee member, investor, philanthropist, father, and husband. He remains one of the most wealthy and powerful men in the world. At the end of 2007 the forty-two-year-old was worth an estimated $17.2 billion and ranked as the eighth-richest person in the United States. He is often asked why, with so many accomplishments behind him and so much money in the bank, he doesn't retire and spend his days relaxing and playing golf. To one such questioner, Michael responded, "I'm having a great time. I take time off and I think I have great balance in my life. But there is only so much fun you can have goofing off. It's a tremendous thrill to be part of an organization like [Dell Inc.] and to see it reach its full potential, and that's massively exciting for me."

Michael Dell
(Courtesy of Dell Inc.)

Timeline

1965   Born February 23 to Alexander and Lorraine Dell, the second of three sons.

1977   Makes $2,000 selling stamps directly to consumers instead of going through auctioneers.

1980   Purchases first computer, an Apple II, and takes it apart to understand how it works.

1982   Earns $18,000 selling newspaper subscriptions.

1983   Begins selling upgraded PCs and computer parts out of dorm room at University of Texas.

1984   With $1,000 in start-up money, registers business in March under the name PC's Limited; drops out of the University of Texas in May.

1986   Unveils the industry's then fastest-performing computer at the time.

1987   Establishes Dell UK, eleven more overseas operations open in the next four years; receives Austin area Technology Award; limited sale of stock raises $21.5 million.

1988   Dell Computer Corporation goes public, raising $30 million in initial public offering.

1989 Receives the advertising firm Ernst & Young's "Entrepreneur of the Year" award; marries Susan Lieberman.

1990 Receives *Inc.* magazine's "Entrepreneur of the Year" award.

1992 Becomes youngest CEO of a company to earn a ranking on the Fortune 500; wins "Person of the Year" award from *PC Magazine*.

1994 Launches the Latitude XP notebook line, containing lithium-ion batteries; launches Web site www.dell.com, and begins taking orders over the Internet.

1998 Dell overtakes IBM to become the third-largest supplier of notebook computers in the United States.

1999 Establishes the Michael and Susan Dell Foundation, a charitable organization with an endowment of more than $1 billion; writes autobiography and management handbook *Direct from Dell: Strategies that Revolutionized an Industry.*

2001 Dell Computer becomes the world's largest PC maker, overtaking computer rival Compaq.

2004 Steps down as CEO of Dell, but remains chairman of the board.

2006 Dell Inc. suffers through problems, including a massive recall of dangerous laptop batteries and an investigation by the Securities and Exchange Commission (SEC); loses top spot in global PC sales to resurgent Hewlett-Packard.

2007 Retakes position as CEO in January, after Kevin Rollins tenders his resignation.

Sources

CHAPTER ONE: A Business-Minded Boy

p. 11, "I learned an early . . ." Michael Dell and Catherine Fredman, *Direct from Dell: Strategies that Revolutionized an Industry* (New York: HarperCollins, 1999), 4.

p. 12, "In our household . . ." Ibid., 3.

p. 12, "It's not like I had . . . " Ibid., xvi.

p. 14, "I was kind of fascinated . . ." Tom Krazit, "Dell Reflects on 25 Years of PCs," *CNET News.com*, August 7, 2006, http://news.com.com/2009-1042-6099132.html.

p. 15, "[I was] just fascinated . . . very exciting time," Ibid.

p. 17, "make more money . . ." Claire Poole, "The kid Who Turned Computers into Commodities," *Forbes,* October 21, 1999, 318.

p. 18, "Where I come from . . ." Dell and Fredman, *Direct from Dell*, 13.

CHAPTER TWO: Young Man, Young Company

p. 19, "I liked Chinese food . . ." Stanley W. Angrist, "Entrepreneur in Short Pants," *Forbes,* March 7, 1988, 84.

p. 20, "I was fortunate . . ." Michael Dell, "Remarks at

University of Texas at Austin," 2003, http://www.dell.
com/downloads/global/corporate/speeches/msd/2003_
05_17_msd_commencement.pdf.

p. 21, "You've got to stop . . .with IBM!" Dell and
Fredman, *Direct from Dell*, 10.

p. 21, "I knew that if you took . . ." Ibid.

p. 23, "I just went ahead . . ." Nancy F. Koehn, *Brand New:
How Entrepreneurs Earned Consumers' Trust from
Wedgwood to Dell* (Boston: Harvard Business
School Publishing, 2001), 13.

p. 23, "Though I left . . ." Dell, "Remarks at University
of Texas at Austin."

p. 23-24, "I was in college . . ." Charles Fishman,
"Face Time with Michael Dell," *Fast Company,*
February 2001, 82.

p. 24, "manufacturing consisted of . . ." Dell and
Fredman, *Direct from Dell*, 13.

p. 25, "It became very obvious . . ." Poole, "The Kid
Who Turned Computers into Commodities," 318.

p. 26, "We outgrew our telephone systems . . ." Dell
and Fredman, *Direct from Dell*, 19.

p. 26, "When I started . . ." Ibid., 18.

p. 27, "Why are you wasting . . ." John Pletz, "Michael
Dell's View From the Top," *Austin American-Statesman,*
May 2, 2004, http://www.statesman.com/business/
content/business/stories/archive/0502dell.html.

p. 27, "just another soon-to-flame-out hotshot," Angrist,
"Entrepreneur in Short Pants," 84.

p. 29, "I didn't know . . ." Mike Marriner, Nathan Gebhard,
and Joanne Gordon, *Roadtrip Nation: A Guide to*

Discovering Your Path in Life (New York: Ballantine Books, 2003), 133.

CHAPTER THREE: Making Dell Different

p. 31, "In one swoop . . ." Joan Magretta, ed., *Managing in the New Economy* (Boston: Harvard Business School Publishing, 1999), 193.

p. 31, "When the company started . . ." Ibid., 195.

p. 32, "Lee helped me . . ." Poole, "The Kid Who Turned Computers into Commodities," 318.

p. 32, "Michael didn't want his name . . ." Pletz, "Michael Dell's View from the Top."

p. 34, "Of all the people . . ." Ibid.

p. 34, "Very few business managers . . ." Koehn, *Brand New: How Entrepreneurs Earned Consumers' Trust from Wedgwood to Dell,* 276.

p. 34, "They probably didn't . . ." Dell and Fredman, *Direct from Dell,* 19.

p. 37, "Our close connection . . ." Ibid., 139.

p. 37, "We began receiving . . ." Ibid., 25–26.

p. 39, "I observed the same . . ." Ibid., 28.

p. 40, "Sometimes it's better . . ." Ibid., 12.

p. 42, "investors had real faith . . ." Ibid., 32.

p. 43, "Most men I dated . . ." Pamela Colloff, "Suddenly Susan," *Texas Monthly,* August 2000, 124.

p. 44, "When you were talking . . ." Pletz, "Michael Dell's View From the Top."

CHAPTER FOUR: Ups and Downs

p. 46, "We bought as many . . ." Dell and Fredman, *Direct from Dell,* 36.

p. 47, "the company's biggest . . ." Koehn, *Brand New:*

How Entrepreneurs Earned Consumers' Trust from Wedgwood to Dell, 314.

p. 47, "'Some things are compelling . . .'" Dell and Fredman, *Direct from Dell*, 38.

p. 47-48, "We made some mistakes . . ." Banning Kent Lary, "An 'Instinct' for Computer Success," *Nation's Business*, April 1991, 46.

p. 50, "We could not sell . . ." Dell and Fredman, *Direct from Dell*, 51.

p. 50, "Michael was mortified . . ." Pletz, "Michael Dell's View From the Top."

p. 52, "We'd have meetings . . ." Dan McGraw, "The Kid Bytes Back," *U.S. News and World Report*, December 12, 1994, 70.

p. 54, "In early 1993 . . ." Dell and Fredman, *Direct from Dell*, 50.

p. 54, "Today people sometimes ask . . ." Ibid., 38.

p. 55, "Because we laid out . . ." Ibid., 53.

p. 55, "Energy power systems . . ." Ibid., 54.

p. 57, "Dell had the opportunity . . ." Dell, "Remarks at University of Texas at Austin."

CHAPTER FIVE: Racing at the Speed of "Dell-ocity"

p. 59, "One of the things . . ." Jacob Rahul, "The Resurrection of Michael Dell," *Fortune*, September 18, 1995, 117.

p. 62, "I didn't know everything . . ." Koehn, *Brand New: How Entrepreneurs Earned Consumers' Trust from Wedgwood to Dell*, 304.

p. 62, "He didn't try to run . . ." Pletz, "Michael Dell's View From the Top."

p. 62, "I'm fearful all the time," Colloff, "Suddenly Susan," 124.

p. 63, "The house is a place . . ." Helen Thorpe, "Michael Dell," *Texas Monthly,* September 1997, 117.

p. 63-64, "I was enthralled by the concept . . ." Dell and Fredman, *Direct from Dell*, 89.

p. 64-65, "If you could order . . ." Ibid., 88.

p. 65, "Dell has been positioned . . ." Koehn, *Brand New: How Entrepreneurs Earned Consumers' Trust from Wedgwood to Dell*, 316.

p. 67, "For Dell, the online world . . ." Gary McWilliams, "Michael Dell: Whirlwind on the Web," *Business Week*, April 7, 1997, http://www.businessweek.com/1997/14/b3521131.htm.

p. 69, "I don't think Michael . . . " Andrew E. Serwer, "Michael Dell Turns the PC World Inside Out," *Fortune*, September 8, 1997, 76.

p. 71, "The first reason . . ." Thorpe, "Michael Dell," 119.

CHAPTER SIX: Reaching the Top

p. 75-76, "A bunch of . . ." Pletz, "Michael Dell's View From the Top."

p. 76, "Giving isn't just . . ." Jennifer Karlin, "The Mother Jones 400: Michael S. Dell (with Susan)," *Mother Jones.com*, March 5, 2001, http://www.motherjones. com/news/special_reports/mojo_400/104_dell.html.

p. 78, "We understand that some . . ." Ibid.

p. 78, "enable the President to . . ." *President's Council of Advisors on Science and Technology*, http://www.ostp. gov/PCAST/pcast.html.

p. 78, "serves as a catalyst . . ." *The President's Council on Physical Fitness and Sports*, http://www.fitness.gov/home_about.htm.

p. 79, "set your sights . . ." Dell, "Remarks at University of Texas at Austin."

p. 79, "Occasionally, rarely, history . . ." Koehn, *Brand New: How Entrepreneurs Earned Consumers' Trust from Wedgwood to Dell*, 261.

p. 79, "brilliantly and intuitively . . ." Fons Trompenaars and Charles Hampden-Turner, *21 Leaders for the 21st Century* (New York: McGraw-Hill, 2002), 243.

p. 79, "It's like watching . . ." Andrew Park and Peter Burrows, "What You Don't Know About Dell," *Business Week*, November 3, 2003, http://www.businessweek.com/magazine/content/03_44/b3856001_mz001.htm.

p. 80, "First, Dell steers customers . . . " Daniel Lyons, "Michael Dell's Second Act," *Forbes,* April 17, 2000, 208.

p. 81, "Adding $7 billion . . ." Lisa Gibbs, "Is Dell's Ride Over?" *Money,* November 1, 2000, 35.

p. 81, "He had more to lose . . ." Pletz, "Michael Dell's View From the Top."

p. 81, "We're a growth company . . ." Ibid.

p. 83, "Your competitors want this deal . . ." Kathryn Jones, "Together at Last: After Eight Months of Wrangling, Compaq and Hewlett-Packard Have Joined Forces. What Does the Motherboard of All Mergers Mean for Texas?" *Texas Monthly*, June 2002, 78.

p. 83, "More and more doors . . . ." Ibid., 79.

p. 84, "I've still got the same . . ." David Kirkpatrick, "Dell and Rollins: The $41 Billion Buddy Act," *Fortune,* April 19, 2004, 84.

p. 84-85, "People don't realize . . ." Ibid.

CHAPTER SEVEN: A Private Man

p. 86, "I don't have any desire . . ." Thorpe, "Michael Dell," 117.

p. 87, "I like any good . . ." Pletz, "Michael Dell's View From the Top."

p. 87, "an in-your-face desire . . ." Ibid.

p. 88, "He is extremely family-oriented . . ." Marie Lingblom, "Top 25 Executives: Michael Dell," *CRN. com*, November 7, 2001, http://www.crn.com/it-channel/18827436.

p. 89, "It was powerful stuff . . ." Park and Burrows, "What You Don't Know About Dell."

p. 89, "bogeyman of the PC . . ." Pletz, "Michael Dell's View From the Top."

p. 89, "It's the biggest, baddest . . ." Ibid.

p. 89, "There's no 'The dog ate . . ." Park and Burrows, "What You Don't Know About Dell."

p. 89, "It's not relevant . . ." Fishman, "Face Time with Michael Dell," 82.

p. 90, "It's fun to do things . . ." Dell and Fredman, *Direct from Dell*, 33.

p. 90, "Believe in what . . ." Ibid., 29.

p. 90, "Probably the smartest thing . . ." Angrist, "Entrepreneur in Short Pants," 84.

p. 91, "Try never to be . . ." Dell, "Remarks at University of Texas at Austin."

p. 92, "Dell produces an awful lot . . ." Fishman, "Face Time with Michael Dell," 83.

p. 92, "I go to the Usenet forums . . ." Ibid.

p. 93, "The Foundation's mission . . ." "Dell Scholars,"

Michael and Susan Dell Foundation, http://www.dell scholars.org/programoverview.aspx.

p. 95, "It's really easy . . ." Jill Rosenfeld, "Giving Back," *Fast Company,* November 1999, 109.

p. 95-96, "I'm a pretty results-oriented . . ." Pletz, "Michael Dell's View From the Top."

p. 97, "Michael Dell has changed . . ." "Michael Dell to Receive CEA's Digital Patriots Award at March 27 Dinner," *BusinessWire*, October 18, 2006, http://dvd. consumerelectronicsnet.com/articles/viewarticle. jsp?id=74847.

p. 97, "There's always a better . . ." Dell, "Remarks at University of Texas at Austin."

CHAPTER EIGHT: Back in Charge

p. 101, "Our business in North America . . ." Andy Serwer, "The Education of Michael Dell," *Fortune*, March 7, 2005, 72.

p. 102, "You have to just say . . ." Ibid.

p. 104, "We know exactly why . . ." Tom Espiner, "Michael Dell: Exploding Batteries are Sony's Fault," ZD Net UK, September 16, 2006, http://michael-dell-news. newslib.com/story/7569-82/.

p. 104, "White smoke began to pour . . ." Louisa Hearn, "Dell laptop became a flamethrower," *Sydney Morning Herald*, July 31, 2006, http://www.smh.com.au/news/ laptops--desktops/laptop-turns-to-flamethrower/2006/ 07/28/1153816375720.html.

p. 105, "I'm now so paranoid . . ." Hearn, "Dell laptop became a flamethrower."

p. 105, "Customers can always . . ." Sandra Rossi, "Dell Founder has little to say," *Network World*, August 15, 2006, http://www.networkworld.com/news/2006/081506-dell-founder-has-little-to.html.

p. 106, "It's becoming harder . . ." Nanette Byrnes, Peter Burrows, and Louise Lee, "Dark Days at Dell," *Business Week*, August 24, 2006, http://www.businessweek.com/technology/content/aug2006/tc20060823_809079.htm.

p. 107, "one mishap after another," Byrnes, Burrows, and Lee, "Dark Days at Dell."

p. 108, "Michael's vision and leadership . . ." Dell Inc., "Michael Dell Assumes Duties as Chief Executive Officer of Dell Inc.," press release, January 31, 2007, http://www.dell.com/content/topics/global.aspx/corp/pressoffice/ en/2007/2007_01_31_rr_000?c=us&l=en&s=corp.

p. 108, "The direct model . . ." David Whitford, "Uh . . . Maybe I Should Drive," *Fortune*, April 30, 2007, 124.

p. 109, "What you are going . . ." Krazit, "Dell Reflects on 25 years of PCs."

p. 109, "I'm having a great time . . ." "Dell us the Answer: More Questions for Michael Dell," Always-On Network, January 26, 2004, http://www.alwayson-network.com/comments.php?id=P2578_0_4_0_C.

Bibliography

Angrist, Stanley W. "Entrepreneur in Short Pants."
Forbes, March 7, 1988.

Byrnes, Nanette, Peter Burrows, and Louise Lee. "Dark
Days at Dell." *BusinessWeek*, August 24, 2006. http://
www.businessweek.com/technology/content/aug2006/
tc20060823_809079.htm.

Colloff, Pamela. "Suddenly Susan." *Texas Monthly,*
August 2000.

Dell Inc. "Michael Dell Assumes Duties as Chief
Executive Officer of Dell Inc." Press release, January
31, 2007. http://www.dell.com/content/topics/global.
aspx/corp/pressoffice/en/2007/2007_01_31_rr_000?
c=us&l=en&s=corp.

Dell, Michael. *Direct from Dell: Strategies that
Revolutionized an Industry.* New York: Harper-
Collins, 1999.

———. "Remarks at University of Texas at Austin."
Keynote address, commencement ceremony at the
University of Texas, Austin, May, 15, 2003. http://www.

dell.com/downloads/global/corporate/speeches/msd/2003_
05_17_msd_commencement.pdf.

Michael and Susan Dell Foundation. "Dell Scholars."
http://www.dellscholars.org/programoverview.aspx.

Espiner, Tom. "Michael Dell: Exploding Batteries are
com, November 7, 2001. http://www.crn.com/it-channel/
18827436.

Lyons, Daniel. "Michael Dell's Second Act." *Forbes,* April
17, 2000.

Magretta, Joan, ed., *Managing in the New Economy.*
Boston: Harvard Business School Press, 1999.

Marriner, Mike, Nathan Gebhard, and Joanne Gordon.
*Roadtrip Nation: A Guide to Discovering Your Path in
Life.* New York: Ballantine Books, 2003.

McGraw, Dan. "The Kid Bytes Back." *U.S. News and
World Report,* December 12, 1994.

McWilliams, Gary. "Michael Dell: Whirlwind on the
Web." *BusinessWeek*, April 7, 1997. http://www.business
week.com/1997/14/b3521131.htm.

"Michael Dell to Receive CEA's Digital Patriots Award
at March 27 Dinner." *Business Wire*, October 18, 2006.

Park, Andrew, and Peter Burrows. "What You Don't
Know About Dell." *BusinessWeek*, November 3, 2003.
http://www.businessweek.com/magazine/content/03_
44/b3856001_mz001.htm.

Pletz, John. "Michael Dell's View From the Top."
Austin American-Statesman, May 2, 2004. http://www.
statesman.com/business/content/business/stories/archive/
0502dell.

Poole, Claire. "The kid Who Turned Computers into
Commodities." *Forbes,* October 21, 1999.

Rahul, Jacob. "The Resurrection of Michael Dell." *Fortune,*
September 18, 1995.

Rossi, Sandra. "Dell Founder has little to say."
Network World, August 15, 2006. http://www.net
workworld.com/news/2006/081506-dell-founder-has-
little-to.html.

Serwer, Andrew E. "The Education of Michael Dell."
Fortune, March 7, 2005.

———. "Michael Dell Turns the PC World Inside Out."
Fortune, September 8, 1997.

Thorpe, Helen. "Michael Dell." *Texas Monthly,*
September 1997.

Trompenaars, Fons, and Charles Hampden-Turner. *21
Leaders for the 21st Century: How Innovative Leaders
Manage in the Digital Age.* New York: McGraw
Hill, 2002.

Whitford, David. "Uh . . . Maybe I Should Drive."
Fortune, April 30, 2007.

Web sites

http://www.msdf.org
This site contains a wealth of information about the charitable activities of the Michael and Susan Dell Foundation, started by Michael and his wife in 1999.

http://www.dell.com
Dell's home page provides numerous links to current products and equipment made by Dell.

http://michael-dell-news.newslib.com
Visitors to this site will find a useful collection of articles and updates on new developments in Michael Dell's professional life.

http://www.forbes.com
The Web site of *Forbes*, a prominent business magazine that contains news on Michael Dell and other business figures. Includes annual salary and net worth rankings.

http://www.businessweek.com
BusinessWeek.com, the online version of *BusinessWeek* magazine, contains important information about the computer industry and other topics related to Michael Dell.

Index